PRACTICAL HINTS

ON

CAMPING

BY
HOWARD HENDERSON

FOREWORD BY
VIN T. SPARANO

Racehorse Publishing

First published in 1882 by Jansen, McClurg and Company

First Racehorse Publishing Edition 2017

All rights to any and all materials in copyright owned by the publisher are strictly reserved by the publisher.

Foreword © 2017 Vin T. Sparano

Racehorse Publishing books may be purchased in bulk at special discounts for sales promotion, corporate gifts, fund-raising, or educational purposes. Special editions can also be created to specifications. For details, contact the Special Sales Department, Skyhorse Publishing, 307 West 36th Street, 11th Floor, New York, NY 10018 or info@skyhorsepublishing.com.

Racehorse Publishing™ is a pending trademark of Skyhorse Publishing, Inc.®, a Delaware corporation.

Visit our website at www.skyhorsepublishing.com.

10 9 8 7 6 5 4 3 2 1

Library of Congress Cataloging-in-Publication Data is available on file.

Cover design by Lori Wendin
Cover artwork credit: iStockphotos

Print ISBN: 978-1-944686-38-3
Ebook ISBN: 978-1-944686-40-6

Printed in the United States of America

TO

GEORGE VAN ZANDT,

MY STEADFAST FRIEND.

CONTENTS

PREFACE.

THE camper has of late years occupied a distinctive position by the side of the hunter, the angler and the canoeist. Each summer adds to the number of those who, without being expert in the arts of the sportsman, go out for the mere pleasure of camping. Even ladies and children penetrate the depths of our forests, share in the genial glow of the camp-fire, and enhance the pleasure of a woodland life by their presence. The lover of nature, the artist, the sportsman and the naturalist, each find occupation, amusement and rest.

The aim in writing this little work has been to give concisely some practical hints sufficient for guidance, which can be acted upon according to the length of the purse and the degree of one's enthusiasm. Whether the reader's tent be pitched upon the seashore, beside a mountain brook, or upon the rolling prairie, it is hoped that something may be found in the following pages which will add to his comfort and his pleasure.

For the kindness of authors and publishers in allowing extracts to be taken from their works, for which credit will be found elsewhere, thanks are due.

FOREWORD

I'VE BEEN a camper, hunter, and fisherman all my life and I hate to admit it, but modern technology has spoiled us rotten. When we head into the woods, we like to think of ourselves as mountain men and women, tough woodsmen who can survive in the bush and live off the land. A quick look in my backpack tells me a much different story. I carry a smartphone, a handheld GPS, a space blanket in case I get chilly, a fire starter that I simply squirt on a wet log and conjure a roaring campfire, and high-energy power bars in case I get hungry. My clothes and boots are waterproof and windproof. My tent literally pops up in seconds. When we tell friends that we're roughing it in the woods, we should bite our tongues.

When I was asked to take a look at this book, I wondered what was left to say about an activity made quite comfortable by L.L. Bean and the Bass Pro stores. But then I saw that this book was published in 1882, long before the creation of the outdoor gear that we take for granted today. What I discovered in its pages is fascinating reading about what camping was like nearly 135 years ago.

I already told you what's in *my* backpack, but now let's go back in time. In 1882, here are a few of the items Henderson tells us to put in our packs. He recommends heavy flannel shirts, stout woolen pantaloons, French kip-skin boots, Balmoral shoes, pipes and tobacco, Indian blankets, and a pair of buckskin gauntlets. The author even suggests you make a blanket bag out of "ordinary grain bags."

It's interesting to wonder what Henderson would have thought if he walked through one of our outdoor stores today. I kept comparing his grand-old advice to the gear I see in my Cabela's catalog. It was like reading about the 1804 Lewis and Clark expedition and the tortuous conditions they encountered. Too bad Lewis and Clark didn't have a copy of Henderson's book. It might have kept them out of trouble.

Keep in mind that back in 1882, we still had a long way to go with our medical knowledge. Penicillin and antibiotics weren't developed until the early 1920s. Any kind of injury or wounds on a camping trip meant a serious risk of infection. So what kind of camping advice would an outdoor writer offer 135 years ago? Not knowing what the future held, Henderson's recommended treatment of a wound is a little scary:

"Bleeding from a wound on man or beast may be stopped by a mixture of wheat flour and common salt, in equal parts, bound on with a cloth. If the bleeding be profuse, use a large quantity, say from one to three pints. It may be left on for hours, or even days, if necessary."

If I cut myself on a camping trip, I doubt I'd mix up a batch of salt-laden wheat flour and put it on my wound. I'll opt for some Neosporin and a sterile bandage. Although reading Henderson's sage advice at a time when trekking into the woods could well be risky, his ideas might have saved lives during the time. I do, however, take issue with the author's treatment for snakebite. Although not a cure, I do confess that his treatment might relieve some tension. Henderson suggests "For the bite of a rattlesnake, whisky taken freely seems to be the only antidote."

I still found the author's book a valuable insight, even if some of his advice might sound outdated today. How else can we appreciate what we have today without first acknowledging our past? Henderson gave us safe and sound advice more than 135 years ago and we owe him a debt of gratitude. Reading his wonderful little book gives us a great deal of insight into the world of camping and offers us fascinating comparisons to the modern camper.

I wonder how many campers today would venture into the woods and waters equipped with only Henderson's gear and advice. You can start out by leaving your geodesic tent, your cell phone, and GPS at home. Do you know how to build a lean-to? You can leave the trail, but do you still remember how to use a map and compass? If you don't have a compass, Henderson reminds us that moss is thickest in the shade on the north side of the trees and the branches of a tree are the largest on the south side. How's that for trail-blazing?

Want to take the challenge and go into the woods with the gear Horace Henderson used 135 years ago? Good luck. You may quickly discover that you may not be as tough as Horace. Make sure you take his little book with you.

—Vin T. Sparano, Editor Emeritus, *Outdoor Life*; author of *The Complete Outdoors Encyclopedia* and *The Complete Guide to Camping and Wilderness Survival*

PRACTICAL HINTS ON CAMPING.

CHAPTER I.

PREPARATION.

A RECENT writer has well said that the genuine camper divides the year by the 1st of January. Up to that time his talk is all about the last camp he had, and after that it is all of the next camp. The old adage "Seize time by the forelock, for he is bald behind," applies as well to pleasure as to business. Double is the enjoyment to the lover of woodland life if he knows weeks ahead just when, and just where, he is going to spend his vacation. Nor can he too early in the season look over and perfect his kit. Many an hour's dearly bought pleasure has been marred by simply not preparing in time. The camper should always bear in mind that homely phrase, and "get a good ready." Make out a full inventory of all you have on hand which you may want for the next vacation. Put down everything; not only usual cooking utensils, clothing, tent, and fishing tackle, but also the little odds and ends of things, such as a chain, a hook, a piece of wire, etc. Often these little trifles prove a most valuable part of your inventory. Put down each article in a line by itself. Do not jumble three or four items together. Having completed your inventory, make out a supplementary inventory of all those things which past experience has taught you the necessity of, or which you think you require, and you have not already on your list. Leave nothing to memory; put every article down. Next read everything you can find referring to camping; and especially is this important if you are a novice, for good camping is an art to be acquired only by experience and careful attention to every detail. One man will have twice the comfort, twice the pleasure, and at one-half the expense, that another man will, simply by knowing how to camp. As you read, make notes, and add to your supplementary inventory such articles as you find you have overlooked.

Examine your lists carefully and strike out everything you think you can get along without. Simplicity should be your constant aim. Dispense with all the requirements of city life as far as possible. If you are inexperienced, you probably will find after one or two seasons out, that of the articles you took with you into the woods the first time, you could have left two-thirds of them at home, and still have been very well provided.

While accumulating information, decide how you are going to carry your things. Much of your stuff can be packed as well at once as later. Often the first care of an old camper after his return, is to put everything in order for the next season. Every article relating to camp life, except perhaps clothing, should be kept by itself. How to pack is a problem each must settle for himself. Boxes with hinged covers will be found very useful, though perhaps good strong trunks are better than anything else. They are more easily handled in camp, and go as personal baggage *en route;* thus obviating the necessity, at times, of sending part of your kit ahead by freight. You will find it convenient to know the weight of each piece of baggage, and it will assist you in making future plans.

Travel as light as possible, but be sure you have sufficient clothing and bedding to keep warm. A heavy double blanket, and two rubber blankets, one beneath you and one over you, will generally be found sufficient for the night. Besides usual clothing you should have one set of light summer, and one set of heavy winter underwear. A light flannel wrapper, or vest, should always be worn.

Provisions should be packed entirely by themselves. Do not undertake to do it yourself, even for small purchases. Go to some large grocery house, and their packer will put up your things neater and better than you can. They will furnish a suitable box, and see that it is properly marked. You can also generally obtain from them a printed price-list which you will find advantageous in helping you decide what you want. But — beware — take care — make it a condition precedent to your purchase that you are to oversee the wrapping up of every package, and to check off yourself every article as it is put in the box. Be not deceived by any assurances whatever. This is important, and something *you must attend to yourself*. It is no slight matter to be from ten to forty miles from a settlement and find you are minus the fish-sauce, or that the pepper or salt has been forgotten. Have everything double wrapped. Better still, use small bags. Coin bags of different sizes, such as bankers use, will be found for many things very convenient. Do not forget to ask for an old meal bag. It is one of the most serviceable articles in camp. Take a bill of your purchases, and examine it carefully and preserve it. Old grocery bills are frequently valuable to refer to.

Provisions can be left to the last, but all other purchases should have been completed days before. Allow ample time for every preparation. Do not fly around town the last morning like a decapitated hen. You will find enough to annoy one in camp; and you should start out as calmly and quietly as you *go down to your business.

A cheap flexible blank book, which can be carried in the side pocket, will be found very convenient. It should be of about twenty-four pages, the ruling narrow, and the page wide. Such a book which came under our notice was filled out as follows :

INVENTORY OF ARTICLES BELONGING TO A. B.

CLOTHING.

CAMP EQUIPAGE.

HUNTING OUTFIT.

FISHING TACKLE.

Under this last head were enumerated the different lines, giving size and length of each, the number of hooks and their sizes ; the number of flies, giving the kind, size, color and price of each, etc., etc.

MISCELLANEOUS ARTICLES.

PRIVATE EXPENSE ACCOUNT.

EXPENSES IN COMMON.

Memorandum.

Left ——— on a camping expedition ——— 188 — at —— o'clock –m., via ———————. Party numbers —— as follows : ———. Reached camp at —— o'clock

—m., on the —— day of ———, 188-. Broke camp
————. Reached home————, 188-. Time
absent ————. Total cost of trip, $———.

NOTES.

Here follow various entries; such as notes of travel,
observations, practical hints, a running diary of the
trip, etc.

Such a book, by properly checking off the inventory,
may last for two or three seasons; or if preferred you
can get a new one each year for a few cents, and thus
have an interesting volume relating to each expedition.

Avoid dressing "loud." Buy a cheap suit, or better
still, wear your old clothes. Dark colors are preferable, being less liable to attract the attention of
game, and easier to take care of. Rubber boots, except for ladies, are not recommended. For rubber
blankets take the government poncho. It will be
found very convenient. A rubber coat is very serviceable at times, but is not indispensable. Boots should
be very easy, and take along an old pair of slippers.
A hammock will be found enjoyable. A cheap one
will do, but do not take the smallest adult size; it is
not quite large enough for real comfort.

Be sure you take with you a large stock of patience
and good nature. Camping out tests the character.
A good camper accommodates himself to circumstances, and is too much of a philosopher to con-

descend to quarrel. Make no rules, if you can avoid it, and break none that are made. If you are appointed a leader, shift the office upon the shoulders of another man if you can ; and if not, then govern by tact and quiet influence, rather than by arbitrary regulations.

CHAPTER II.

OUTFIT.

WHAT to take in the woods is a question to which a definite answer cannot be given. Much depends upon the size and character of your party, where and how you are going, how long you expect to remain, and whether you are going to a new place, or to some spot with which you are perfectly familiar. The great danger is in carrying too much. You should have an ample supply of blankets and plain food. You require two entire suits of clothing : one suitable for traveling and for general use when not in the woods, and one for exclusive use in camp. Upon reaching camp your traveling suit should be folded and packed away.

In regard to provisions, make out a list of what you propose to take, including tea, coffee, and a few delicacies, then ascertain the total number of pounds in the list. It is safe to estimate that you will require in camp two and a half to three pounds per day to each adult. This includes everything.

If you are not going too far from the confines of

civilization, many things can be purchased near your camp; and if you are an experienced sportsman, some allowance may be made for what you can obtain from your own efforts.

Do not use your condensed soups and canned meats too freely at first. In case of extended trips away from the camp, you will find them convenient to rely upon.

Wallace in his "Guide to the Adirondacks," says:

"Care should be taken to have the outfit light and simple. Don't take too much, and be sure to leave the fancy articles at home. The comfort of the tourist, and especially that of the guide, will be most readily promoted by adhering strictly to this rule. We will name what we consider the essentials: Pair of heavy flannel shirts. Stout woolen pantaloons, coat and vest. Pair of overalls, for night use. Soft felt hat, light color. Two pairs of woolen stockings. Pair of heavy calf-skin or French kip-skin boots, with thick soles and broad heels, one size larger than you usually wear. Balmoral shoes; high cut are better, perhaps, as they support the ankles, and serve to prevent their being sprained. Pair of stout camp (carpet) slippers. Rubber blanket or coat, indispensable. Heavy woolen shawl, or a pair of Indian blankets. A bag is a useful substitute for blankets. It should be made of Canton flannel, or what is preferable, woolen cloth, as it will be less likely to ignite when exposed to fire. It should be about six feet long, and two and a half or three feet wide. We have seen ordinary grain bags used for that purpose, but they afford too contracted a space.

Such a bag can be converted into a knapsack. A pair of light buckskin gauntlets, sufficiently long to button around the elbows. A pair of mits made of long cotton stocking legs will answer as a substitute. Hunting knife and belt. Pint tin cup. Colored silk handkerchief. Head net — a protector from insects. A piece of Swiss mull three or four yards square, will be found of great service, using it as a sort of 'coverlid,' or placing it snugly against the doorway, having previously expelled the insects from the lodge by a thorough smudge. Towels, soap, pins, needles, thread, writing paper, envelopes, postage stamps, pencils, etc., in limited quantities. Hospital stores, including bandages, lint,* ointment, camphor, aqua-ammonia, soda, cholera drops, rhubarb, insect preparation, etc., to use in case of emergency. All the articles enumerated, with the exception of the blankets (which may be strapped outside) can be packed in a common enameled double satchel."

We give the following lists for guidance, but it is not expected that everything mentioned below is to be taken into the woods. Use judgment, and make out your own list. This should not be delayed till the last day, as your list may be subject to many alterations:

---

* "Bleeding from a wound on man or beast may be stopped by a mixture of wheat flour and common salt, in equal parts, bound on with a cloth. If the bleeding be profuse, use a large quantity, say from one to three pints. It may be left on for hours, or even days, if necessary."

GENTLEMAN'S OUTFIT.

Two suits of clothes,
Two light wrappers,
One winter wrapper,
Two pairs of light drawers,
One pair of winter drawers,
Two flannel shirts,
Bathing suit or trunks,
Two pairs of soft woolen socks,
Two pairs of light socks for traveling,
Collars and cuffs,
A white shirt or two,
A large scarf,
One pair of boots,
One pair of shoes,
One pair of slippers,
Overcoat,
Rubber overcoat, or poncho,
Felt hat,
Toilet soap,
Towels,
Comb,
Tooth brush,
Small looking-glass,
Folding drinking cup.

Pipes and tobacco,
Matches,
Medicine,
Raw cotton for cuts and wounds,
Insect preventive,
Maps,
Pocket flask,
Guide-book,
Compass,
Stamps and stamped envelopes,
Plain envelopes,
Postal cards,
Lead pencils,
Aniline pencil or pen,
Pens, ink, paper,
Strong pocket knife,
Blacking and brush,
Clothes brush,
Wisp broom,
Portfolio,
Small size Bible,
Money,
Watch and key,
Whistle.

LADY'S OUTFIT.

Look over the gentleman's list, and in addition to the articles mentioned there which you may require, the following are suggested :

Traveling dress,
Short walking dress, dark flannel,
Flannel underclothing,
Soft felt hat,
Heavy soled boots (easy),

Flannel night-dress (very convenient for cold weather),
Thick, strong gloves,
Gauntlets reaching to the elbow to protect from insects,

Rubber overshoes,
Rubber boots,
Light rubber waterproof and cap,
Warm waterproof.

Air pillow,
Toilet articles,
Shawl.

KITCHEN UTENSILS AND TABLE SERVICE.

Two frying pans,
Iron kettle, or large tin pail with lid.
Stew pan with cover,
Coffee pot (better with a lip and bail),
Small tin pails,
Kitchen knife,
Large fork with long handle,
Knives and forks,
Table spoons,
Tea spoons,
Two can openers.

Half-pint tin cups, one for each person, and one or two extra,
Deep tin pans for baking,
Tin plates for all, and three or four extra,
Several large iron spoons with long handles,
Dipper,
Dish cloths,
Tea towels,
Camp stove,
Soap.

MISCELLANEOUS LIST.

Axe,
Hatchet,
Hooks,
Nails,
Tacks,
Screws,
Screw drivers,
File,
Awl,
Saw,
Piece of light copper wire,
Spade,
Chalk,
Fishing tackle,
Rifle,
Shot gun,
Ammunition,

Padlock with two keys,
Chain for boat,
Chain for fireplace,
Camp chairs,
Folding cot-bed,
Tent,
Tent poles,
Tent pins,
Hammock,
Rope,
Stout twine,
Ponchos,
Boat,
Canvas boat,
Lantern and oil,
Wicks,
Candles,

19

Blankets,
Needles,
Sail needles,
Thread,
Pins,
Waxed-ends,
Pieces of leather,
Neat's foot oil.

Matches,
Large sponge for boat,
Patent clothes pins,
Corkscrew,
Meal bag,
Small scales,
Shawl strap.

PROVISIONS.

Coffee,
Tea,
Chocolate,
Extract of Cocoa,
Beans,
Rice,
Oatmeal,
Corn meal,
Flour (self rising, the best),
Crackers,
Ginger snaps,
Hard tack,
Cheese,
Butter,
Lard,
Bacon,
Salt pork,
Herrings,
Mixed pickles,
Chow chow,
Dried fruits,
Vinegar,
Mustard,
Salt (small bag),
Pepper,
Granulated sugar,
Flavoring extracts,
Baking powder,
Yeast.

Soda,
Fish sauce,
Currie,
Olive oil,
Figs,
Macaroni,
(CANNED GOODS).
Lunch ham,
Boned chicken,
Boned turkey,
Curried fowl,
Cooked corn beef.
Roast beef,
Lobster,
Clam chowder,
Fish,
Tomatoes,
Peas,
Beans,
Jellies,
Vermicelli soup,
Julien soup,
Beef soup,
Macaroni soup,
Mock turtle soup,
Extract of beef,
Sardines,
Condensed milk.

See also list and directions in Mr. Gould's work entitled "How to Camp Out."

Two to three tin pails, of from two to three quarts in size, will be found very useful. They should be of different sizes, so that one can fit into the other; this is convenient, not only for packing, but also for cooking certain dishes.

For frying we prefer the old heavy iron pan, although the handle is much shorter and more inconvenient than that of a thin pan. It would be well to take one of each kind.

Do not forget to take plenty of small change.

In regard to provisions, always buy the best of everything.

Campers should not neglect to take a small supply of medicines, such as quinine, laudanum, essence of ginger, camphor, paregoric, etc. Coffee should be kept in tin cans with tight-fitting covers. It is best to take more than one kind of coffee and, perhaps, it would be well to have some mixed. If you use self-rising flour there will be no need of yeast or baking powder. Boots and shoes should be easy, and have inside soles. Use button or laced shoes. If you cannot obtain a coffee pot with a lip, have the spout riveted on, as it is very likely to become unsoldered over a camp fire. Gauntlets are often almost indispensable, as some insects work themselves up under the shirt sleeves and cause intense annoyance. Mosquitoes, black flies, gnats, no-see-ums, etc., abound in many portions of the country. These insects come on in the early spring and follow each other in regular order. By the last of July they are generally gone, and therefore July, August and September are favorite months for camping, though not the best for hunting and fishing. So great is this annoyance from insects at times, that, unless provided against, you are likely to be driven out of the woods entirely.

The most certain insect preventive, and one in great favor with lumbermen, is a mixture of sweet oil and oil of tar; one-fourth of the oil of tar to three-fourths of sweet oil. This we have found effectual. Pour a quantity into the palm of the hand, and rub the hands and arms with it thoroughly. Then, in the same way, apply very freely to the face, neck and ears. A slight application with the tips of the fingers will not suffice. It must be used freely, and will then keep off insects for hours. If this mixture does not work satisfactorily, add a little more of the tar. It is easily washed off, and the tar will keep the skin soft. The odor of tar, is, however, objectionable to many, especially ladies, and we therefore add two receipts which Mr. Wallace vouches for as being "perfectly effective."

(1.) "One-half ounce of oil of pennyroyal poured into three ounces of melted mutton tallow. Lard is sometimes used, but it is too soft, and is not as healing."

(2.) "Six ounces mutton tallow, two ounces camphor, two ounces pennyroyal, one-half ounce creosote (or carbolic acid solution)."

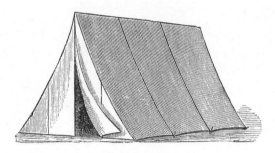

THE A TENT.

THE WALL TENT.

CHAPTER III.

SHELTER.

USE tents for camping. Avoid a hut or shanty, and never sleep in a house, except from necessity. This rule applies to ladies and children, provided they are not very delicate.

The value of the open air, for the night as well as the day, is becoming more and more appreciated. It is a great mistake to think that only men of strong constitutions can stand sleeping in the woods. A recent experiment has shown that during an epidemic, children and adults who were placed in tents, recovered more rapidly, and there was less loss of life among them than among those who remained in their own homes. It is surprising how well nature will take care of you if you will only let her alone. Many a one who toils on from day to day, with weary body, and imagines himself overworked, would feel as fresh and elastic as a boy if he would only sleep with his window *wide* open at night. Not open a little crack so as to create a draft, but wide open so as to prevent a draft and have plenty of fresh air.

Shelter means protection, and whether your walls are twelve inches thick, or the twentieth part of an inch, makes no difference, provided the end sought for is accomplished. In the Adirondacks, and many places in the West, old houses and shanties, built by guides and campers, can be found. You are welcome to use them if not already occupied; but our advice is, to avoid them. Not being in constant use they are often filled with wood vermin, and the timber in them is gradually rotting away, and, combined with the dampness, apt to engender malaria.

The best shelter you can obtain, is that of the ordinary tent. The tents appropriate to your use are the A tent and the wall tent.

It will be seen by reference to the illustrations, that the wall tent is an improvement upon the A tent. The difference is great. The space is better economized. It is far more comfortable; you can dispose of your stuff to better advantage, and you do not have to stand directly on the center line in dressing to avoid striking against the sides, a matter frequently of importance during a heavy rain. A small wall tent is preferable to a large A tent.

The size of the tent depends upon the use you intend to put it to. Take as small a one as will answer with comfort, first, on account of weight, and second, because it is easier to manage. If the party is large, two

A TEMPORARY BARK SHELTER.

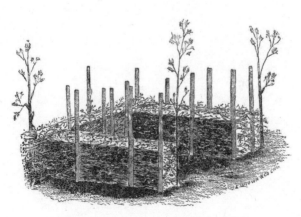

CONSTRUCTION OF A BRUSH HOUSE.

small tents are better than one large one. A wall tent 7 by 9 feet will amply accommodate three with cots, and four without cots.

It will be found very convenient to have a small A tent in which to store luggage and provisions. A tent for cooking is not necessary: you are more likely to burn up your tent than to cook, your dinner. If it storms so that you positively cannot cook (we never met with such an occurrence), why then eat crackers and make fish lines, *and don't growl.* The man who cannot take things philosophically in camp, had better stay at home, and sit in the parlor.

You need not take any tent.* The writer has passed three weeks in the Adirondacks, with a companion, and the whole tent outfit taken into the woods consisted of a piece of strong twine about twelve feet long, and three government ponchos. The weather at times was stormy, but we both kept dry, and neither of us took a cold.

A brush house can be made as follows: cut stakes about eight feet long; drive them into the ground as indicated in the illustration.

Fill in between your stakes with brush. Stamp it down and trim the sides. Cut four forked sticks to

---

* Mr. Charles Hallock, in his admirable work, "The Fishing Tourist," says: "I have slept out three months at a time, and have never used a canvas tent in my life. One who knows how can always make himself comfortable in the woods, even in mid-winter."

support your ridge pole; place the ridge pole in position; throw on the rafters and thatch with fine brush, leaves, grass or hay.

The government poncho makes a good rubber blanket, useful in many ways — as a blanket, a wrap, a cushion, a bag, a sail, etc. etc. There is a slit in the middle, covered by a lapel. In case of rain slip the poncho over your head, and you are protected. It is very light. Carry one around with you at all times, when possible, even if you are off but for a few hours. You never know when you may need it most. It protects you from sudden changes. If overheated, it is convenient as a wrap. If you are chilly put it around you, holding it tight at the throat, and you will soon be warm, for, thin and light as it is, it is air proof as well as water-proof. If fatigued from over-exertion, throw it on the ground, and lie down flat on your back. An eminent medical authority declares that five minutes flat on the back is of more rest to the body than an hour in any other position.

And right here allow a word not strictly pertaining to this chapter. When you are resting, *rest*. Make a business of it. Throw all care and worry, of either home or camp life, off your mind. Do nothing, say nothing, think nothing, be nothing. Recuperate.

To make a poncho tent, cut two stakes of suitable length, with a crotch at one end to hold the ridge pole;

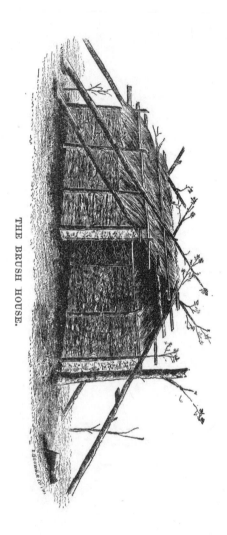

THE BRUSH HOUSE.

cut your ridge-pole and some small stakes or pins.
You will find plenty of suitable material at hand.
Drive your two stakes the length of your poncho apart,
and place your ridge-pole in position, which should be
a little less in height than the width of a poncho.
String two ponchos together by means of the eyelet
holes. Throw them over your ridge-pole — dark side
out — and fasten tightly by the pins and small pieces
of string run through the eyelet holes at the side. A
third poncho protects one end ; the other end is left
open for air and light. This seems very narrow
quarters, but they will sleep two comfortably, and
have been known, by a very slight change, to accommodate three.

If you estimate your tent accommodations by what
you require at home, you will make a mistake. Our
mode of life grants us far more house room than we
require. What an exceedingly small room is a state-
room on any of our boats, and yet it suffices amply for
more than one on a long voyage. If you want to thoroughly realize how very little room you really *need*,
go to an undertaker, and in five minutes he will show
you in what a small space you can lie comfortably.

This simple tent has the advantage of water-proof
sides, is very light, and being in pieces, is easily carried, and can be made and put up inside of twenty
minutes.

There is much gained by placing two logs parallel to each other and setting your poncho tent upon them. This gives far more space than appears at first sight. If you cannot find logs, use small trees, large stones and earth combined.

Select a *cheerful* and *dry* spot for pitching your tent. Choose even ground and slightly sloping. If you expect to remain in camp any length of time, dig, or cut with a hatchet, a small trench around your tent. This will prevent the water from higher ground around you running into your inclosure. If the trees are too thick, make an opening so as to let in the sunshine. Do not thoughtlessly cut down more trees than necessary, and in most cases it will be found easier to find a sufficiently open spot, than to attempt to make one.

Camp as near to a spring, or *running* water, as you can, even though you are on a lake shore.

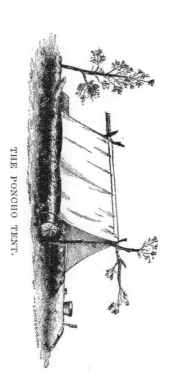

THE PONCHO TENT.

CHAPTER IV.

A FEW GENERAL DIRECTIONS.

AFTER pitching your tent, if you expect to remain at the same spot longer than a day or two, you cannot do better than to devote the next few hours to making your camp as comfortable and pleasant as possible. Put everything in order at once. Do not delay, thinking you can fix up at any time. It is a good plan to stay your tent with extra ropes running from the top of the upright poles. Fasten a number of hooks to your ridge-pole for hanging your clothing at night. If you do not have hooks, you can run a stout line for hanging just below the ridge-pole. See what articles you expect to retain in the tent and what are to be put elsewhere. Select your spot for the camp-fire. If your party is large, or if you have ladies with you, you had better find a few boards, and make a rough table; a couple of boards running parallel with the table will be found more convenient for seats than camp chairs. Dig a good-sized hole for a sink, into which you can throw refuse from your kitchen, and as fast as you throw in anything cover it with a little earth. This will avoid attracting flies and insects. Do not leave parings, old bones and bits from the table lying around upon the ground. Have everything clean and neat around your camp. See that your fire is at a proper distance from your tent and from your table. Do not have these so far from each other as to waste time in walking back and forth. The table should be conveniently near your fire, but not so near as to cause annoyance from the smoke. If possible, store your provisions outside of your tent, but see to it that they are kept dry. Everything should be well covered. Tin cans of all sizes, with tight-fitting covers, will be found most serviceable. Some provisions can be kept in a bag suspended from the limb of a tree, but the bag should be of good thickness to prevent insects from penetrating the cloth.

Unless you camp beside a cool stream, you need a cellar, and a very good one can be made by sinking a barrel. Cover the top with a piece of mosquito netting. Meat and fish can be kept fresh for some time by being salted and hung in a wet bag where it can get the air. Pork can be kept for weeks by putting it in a small tub with half a dozen gimlet holes bored in the bottom to let off the brine. Cover the pork with coarse salt.

A pantry for your dishes can be made by fitting up an old box; or you can easily arrange two or three rustic shelves by driving four strong stakes, to which you nail cross-pieces, and upon these rest short straight sticks cut from a small tree. Cover the whole with a cloth or netting. In driving stakes, etc., do not use the flat side of an axe or hatchet, as it is apt to break the handle.

Have a definite place for toilet duties. Often each one of the party will prefer to select his own particular washing place, but if this is not done, decide upon some general place; and if you can conveniently carry them, it is well before starting to buy several tin wash basins; they are very convenient, although you camp by running water. Each one of the party should have his own soap and towels. A cake of soap can be kept in a little box, around which the towel may be wrapped, and placed in some convenient nook.

You need three clothes-lines. One at the washing place for drying towels, one in your kitchen to be used *exclusively* for dish towels, and one on the outside of the camp for general washing.

For hanging kettles, etc., over the fire, drive two stout forked stakes to support your cross-stick, or set three forked poles. You also need two or three short chains, with hooks at the end.

In the morning open your tent well to air, and if it be a clear day, take out your bedding and hang it in the sun for an hour; do not leave it on the ground.

Unless your tent is very large and your stay protracted, it is hardly worth while to have any flooring for the tent, and instead of strewing hay or straw which is apt to retain moisture, use a plentiful supply of small hemlock twigs, which can generally be found without much trouble. They make a fine green carpet and the odor of them is both pleasant and healthful. Cots are especially necessary for ladies and children, and will add greatly to their comfort and feeling of security. But a healthy person can sleep well on dry ground with impunity. If you do not use a cot, you should have two rubber blankets, one to place on the ground right side down, and the other to throw over you.

It is not advisable to use the hammock for sleeping at night, unless it be a canvas hammock hung within the tent.

The plucking of birds, cleaning of fish, etc., should be done outside of the camp. Do not eat in your tent when it can be avoided.

Be careful not to waste in cooking simply because you have plenty. If, on breaking camp, there is anything of value left, do not throw it away. A neighboring camper or farmer may receive it thankfully. A dead fire with a broken fish pole thrown over it, will probably be considered as a sign that the camp is abandoned, and the next comer is welcome to take what he can find.

If you are camping in deep woods, you need have little fear of anything being stolen by leaving your camp unprotected. Strangers, in passing, generally respect what is called the "law of the woods." And if a straggling hunter should help himself out of your abundance, he will be apt to leave something in its place.

Take with you a small chain and padlock (with two keys) for fastening your boat. This will not prevent the stealing of the boat, but will prevent borrowing, which is almost as inconvenient.

Bathe frequently, but avoid remaining in the water too long, and be careful not to go in when overheated, or immediately after great fatigue. Before diving, ascertain the character of the bottom. "In fording deeply, a heavy stone in the hands, above water, will strengthen your position."

A "smudge" is a small smoky fire, made for driving away insects; you must have little fire and plenty of smoke. See that it is put entirely out when you are through with it, and in all cases be careful not to set fire to the woods. Often immense damage is done by campers in this way. Where the soil is partly made up of vegetable matter, a small fire frequently works a long distance along the ground before it breaks out so as to be perceptible.

If you go on a tramp before breakfast, eat something first, if it be only a cracker. Avoid taking dainties and delicacies in camp. You require plain food that can be easily cooked. The open air and exercise will give a splendid appetite, so that luxuries can be dispensed with. Coffee is strengthening, and good to keep off malaria. Take a little brandy or good whisky, but use it only for medicinal purposes, and be sure then you really *need* it. Liquors of all kinds stimulate, but do not strengthen. There is a general impression among many that something of the kind is needed in camp life, but the best authorities strongly object to their use.

One is not apt to require much medicine in camp. It is advisable, however, to take a variety of the most simple remedies, but in small quantities. Pills are the most convenient. Vials should have the corks tied down tightly and are best kept in place by cutting holes in a piece of pasteboard, which should be secured to short posts glued upon the inside of a small box. Medicines should, for convenience, be kept in one box by themselves, and each bottle or package plainly labeled.

For the bite of a rattlesnake, whisky taken freely seems to be the only antidote. Mr. Joseph W. Long, in his work on "Wild Fowl Shooting," says: "As a local remedy for acute muscular rheumatism, a mustard plaster placed immediately upon the part affected, will, in most cases, soon prove effectual." Reference to camp ailments and the usual medicines required, will be found in another place.

Wherever you camp, even for a night, take your bearings with your pocket compass, and when making any excursion on land do not leave it in the camp, thinking it will not be required. If you lose your way, do not get excited, keep cool, stop a moment to think how you came, and it is generally best to retrace your steps. If you are without a compass, you can be guided somewhat by moss, which, being partial to shade, is the thickest on the north side of the trees. And generally the branches of a tree are the largest on the south side.

Camping tests character; three days in the woods, and all of a man's or woman's individuality crops right out. Good as well as bad traits are apt to be brought out prominently, and to be well defined. In camp, whether the company be large or small, there are those thrown together who are of different tastes, temperaments and dispositions, and who also differ in politics and religion. This close intimacy of tent life, extending over a period of many days, may be one of great unanimity and enjoyment, or of discord and full of petty annoyances. Pleasant and lasting friendships are often formed; so, too, old friends are often alienated.

To thoroughly enjoy camp life, you must take every thing philosophically, even to a dinner of burned beans, seasoned with sand. Then camp cares will be light, camp critics will be silent, camp comforts will be enhanced. Be true to yourself, bear yourself as you do at home, and do not imagine that because you throw off all care, you can throw off all restraint.

Of all things avoid any manifestations of selfishness; remember that your rights are no greater than the rights of others, and frequently there is much gained by yielding your point instead of carrying it by force. Be careful, also, how on the mere strength of a camp acquaintance, you swear eternal friendship to either man or woman.

Without the slightest desire to "preach," we wish to add another word, the result of observation and experience — viz., keep the Sabbath. Let it be a day of rest from pleasure as well as work. Not only should this be done from a proper and gentlemanly regard for the views of others, but the pleasure and duties of camp life so occupy the time that a few hours' quiet rest and a short suspension from the ordinary pursuits of the camp will be found to be of real practical advantage in more ways than one.

A quiet Sunday in the deep woods is a golden day to be remembered for many a year. All nature combines to assist the camper in directing his thoughts to the great Author of all the beauty that he beholds. "The heavens declare the glory of God : and the firmament sheweth his handiwork." The trees under which one reclines rear their heads heavenward, pointing their spire-like minarets far up toward the blue vaulted roof. It inspires the very soul to worship in these unbuilt cathedrals with their wilderness of aisles and pillars, which for elegance and beauty have never been equalled by the architects of any age. And the music of the trees combined with the notes of the bird songsters, give a joy which is unknown in listening to a city choir.

CHAPTER V.

KNOTS AND TIES.

MUCH depends on knowing how to fasten quickly, simply, and thoroughly. We give a description of some of the ties and knots most needed by the camper. They should be studied with a piece of small rope until thoroughly learned, so thoroughly that you can make them naturally, easily, and without stopping to think how they are to be made ; also, make them as they should be made, for often the slightest variation from the correct way is fatal to the security of your knot.

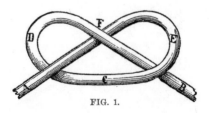

FIG. 1.

SIMPLE KNOT.

A " simple knot," the foundation to all good knots, is made by turning the loose end A, fig. 1, around the body part B, and passing it through its own loop D. Draw tight. The bight D C E separates the two straight parts, which are bound together by the loops D and E.

FIG. 2.

SLIP KNOT.

A "slip knot" is made by tying a "simple knot" around the body part so as to make a third loop, G, Fig. 2, which may be easliy enlarged or diminished by slipping the body part through the "simple knot" part. It is a reliable knot in ordinary strains, if the end of the body part B is properly secured. It is used chiefly in small twines for securing soft packages, bundles of clothing, and similar articles.

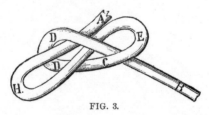

FIG. 3.

SINGLE LOOP KNOT.

A "single loop knot" is the same as the "simple knot," except that the loose end A, Fig. 3, is not drawn entirely through its own loop D.

Observe that both sides of the secondary loop H are on the same side of the primary loop D. It is useful as a "check knot" in many places, in connection with the "slip knot," to secure the running end B, Fig. 2.

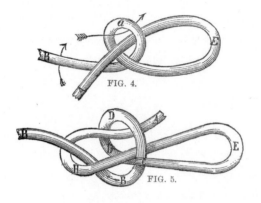

FIG. 4.

FIG. 5.

BOWLINE KNOT.

A "bowline knot" is the same as a "single loop" with the body part B B, Fig. 5, inclosed by the secondary loop H and the primary loop E being drawn well out.

This is a choice knot; so well guarded in all parts that it will never slip, even up to a breaking strain between the primary loop E and the body part B, and is used mainly for fastening by throwing the loop E over a post or stake. It can be made in many ways, and is worthy the attention of any camper who has not already learned its use.

47

To make the "bowline knot," take the rope in your right hand, palm upward, the loose end projecting several inches beyond your right thumb. Take the body part (called the "standing part") similarly in your left hand, palm upward ; the distance between the two hands determines the size of the loop E. With your right hand lay the loose end over the body part beyond the left hand ; with the left hand turn the body part over and around the loose end, so as to inclose it in a circular loop (a, Fig. 4). Hold that loop open and pass the loose end A over the side, down under the body part from left to right, back over the side of the loop, and down through it on the left hand side of the part already there. When you have learned just how to do it, you will use it in preference to all other knots, wherever it is suitable.

A "shank" is used to shorten a line. There are many kinds. Most of them will not endure a severe strain without slipping out. The one shown in Fig. 6 is a "bowline shank," and is perfectly safe.

Take up the slack of the rope and double it in two long bights. Turn each loose end once around the neck of the bight, under itself, and through the bight. If the rope is new and stiff, and subject only to light strains, it may be used without passing the ends through the bights. If the ends are inaccessible, a small loop may be passed through the bight, and a

48

stick placed in the loop ; it will hold, if the stick is firm, under heavy strain.

The ordinary "hard knot" is generally tied as in Fig. 7, which is *wrong;* tighten it, and four times out of

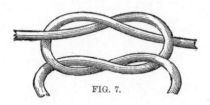

FIG. 7.

five it will slip. This is what sailors call a "granny knot."

Now make your knot as in Fig. 8.

FIG. 8.

SQUARE KNOT, OR REEF KNOT.

You will notice that in the last tie of this knot, Fig. 8, the ends first cross each other *each on its own side,* and *then* turn down and under. This is called a "square knot," and will never slip. Draw tight, and

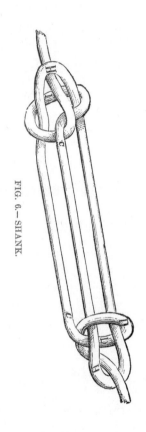

FIG. 6.—SHANK.

notice the difference in shape between this and the granny knot. Always use it at home or in camp.

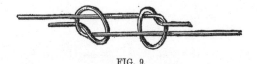

FIG. 9.

FISHERMAN'S KNOT.

A "fisherman's knot" is very convenient for tying the lines together, and is made as shown in the illustration (Fig. 9). After tying, draw your knots together, and cut off the surplus ends.

FIG. 10.

TIMBER HITCH.

A "timber hitch" (Fig. 10) is very useful in towing, or dragging logs and boards.

Pass the end of your rope round the timber, then pass it under and over the standing part, and take several turns around its own part.

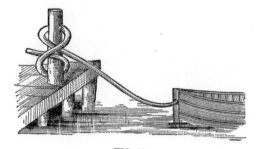

FIG. 11.

CLOVE HITCH.

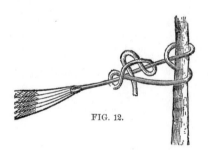

FIG. 12.

HAMMOCK HITCH.

CHAPTER VI.

CAMP COOKING.

THE following observations should be borne in mind : No two campers are likely to cook the same thing in exactly the same way. Each camper is positive that his or her way is the best. Whoever is cook for the time being must quietly pursue his own way with good-natured persistence. If you are not cook, let the cook alone, and attend to your own business. It is excessively annoying while cooking in the open air to have persons sitting around watching, suggesting and criticizing. The responsibility of getting up a dinner for a set of hungry people is in itself sufficient, without any additional perplexities. The cook should always have an abundance of fuel close at hand, both large and small sticks. The one who cooks should never be compelled to collect fire-wood. He must be able to give his whole undivided attention to his special duty.

There are several kinds of portable camp stoves, and a little ingenuity will enable a person to manufacture one for himself from sheet iron. Many who have a permanent camping ground find it very convenient to take out an old-fashioned kitchen wood stove. Ladies not being accustomed to cook by open fire, and on account of the heat and smoke, generally prefer a stove in camp. It is our opinion, however, that after a little experience, taking all things into consideration, an open fire for cooking will be found amply sufficient, especially if the three small fires described below are used.

In regard to the state of the fire for cooking, some prefer the ordinary camp-fire, and others manifest a decided preference for a number of old stumps, which can be used as "back logs," and against which they rest their utensils. Again, some like a large fire, and others a low one. The French cook marvelous dinners over two or three little square holes, filled with burning charcoal, and this has suggested the following method, which experience has proved at times to be most excellent. Have the main fire in a good state, but not too large. Take from it a few live coals, and build three small fires near by, and close to each other. The main part of your dinner is prepared over these small fires. They are more easily kept at a uniform heat; you are much freer from heat and smoke; there is not as much danger of upsetting, and each dish having a distinct fire by itself, there is less confusion. This method will be found not only more convenient, but also has the advantage of cooking a greater number of dishes at the same time, and with little trouble.

T. S. Updegraff suggests a fire-place made as follows: "Pile up a lot of stones, about a foot high and four feet long. Build a wing on each end two feet long. Cover the stones with sod and earth. Now place bars of iron across the top of this upon which to set your cooking utensils."

Iron things should be immediately cleansed as soon as emptied of their contents. They are then hot and the food has not had time to dry and stick. If done at once it will scarcely take a minute, and you will find it not only a great saving of time, but the most disagreeable part of dish-washing will thus be gotten over. If you have not time to wash thoroughly, then scrape and fill them with water and let them stand.

The rule for cleansing cooking utensils as soon as you are through with them applies almost equally well to all other articles connected with the table service. Avoid as far as possible all accumulation of dirty dishes and you will save much time. Never leave anything unwashed till you want to use it again. A rudimentary knowledge of cooking should be acquired at home. The following receipts, however, may be of some value to the camper:

MILK SOUP.—Boil two quarts of milk, with a little salt, a stick of cinnamon, and sugar to sweeten; lay thin slices of toast in a dish, pour over a little milk to soak them, and keep them hot, taking care the milk does not burn. When the soup is ready to serve, beat up the yolks of five eggs, and add them to the milk. Stir it over the fire till it thickens; then take it off lest it curdle, and pour it into the dish upon the toast.

VENISON SOUP.—Three pounds of venison, the inferior pieces will do; one pound ham, or salt pork; one onion; one head of celery (or some celery salt); cut up the meat; chop the vegetables, and put on with just enough water to cover them, keeping the lid on the pot all the while, and stew slowly for one hour. Then add two quarts of boiling water, a few blades of mace, and a little cayenne. Boil two hours longer, salt, and strain. Return the liquor to the pot; stir in a tablespoonful of butter; thicken with a tablespoonful of flour, wet into a smooth, thin paste with cold water; add a tablespoonful of catsup and a tablespoonful of Worcestershire or other pungent sauce.—*Marian Harland.*

RABBIT SOUP.—Cut up the rabbit, crack the bones, and prepare precisely as you would the venison soup, only put in three small onions instead of one, and a bunch of sweet herbs.—*Marian Harland.*

BEAN SOUP.—Soak a quart of beans over night in soft lukewarm water; put them over the fire the next morning with one gallon of cold water, and about two pounds of salt pork. Boil slowly for three hours, keeping the pot well covered; shred into it a head of celery, add pepper, simmer half an hour longer, strain through a colander, and serve.

A good bean soup can be made from the remains of baked beans. Add butter, and a little onion. Boil to a pulp, and strain.

POTATO SOUP.—Peel and cut up four large potatoes, boil them, and when nearly done pour off the water, and add one quart of hot water. Boil two hours, or until the potatoes are thoroughly dissolved. Add fresh boiling water as it boils away. When done, strain, adding three-quarters of a cup of hot cream. Add salt and pepper. Bring to a boiling point, and serve.

FRIED TROUT.—Clean, wash, and dry the fish, roll lightly in flour, and fry in butter, or butter and lard. Let the fat be hot, fry quickly to a delicate brown, and take up the instant they are done. Lay for an instant on a hot folded napkin, to absorb the grease. Serve without seasoning.—*Marian Harland.*

FRIED PICKEREL.—The pickerel ranks next to trout among game fish, and should be fried in the same manner. Take great care not to fry slowly or too long, or the juices and sweetness will be wasted.

FRIED PERCH.—Clean, wash and dry them; salt, and dredge with flour. Have ready a pan of hot lard or butter, put in as many fish as you can without crowding, and fry to a light brown.

FRIED EELS.—Skin them, cut them into four inch lengths, season with salt and pepper, roll them in flour or salted corn meal, and fry them in boiling lard.

BLUEFISH.—This fish is broiled, fried or baked. Prepare for baking by stuffing, and score with a sharp knife to backbone, and insert thin slices of fat pickled pork. For broiling, split down the back.

FRIED VENISON COLLOPS.—Cut nice steaks. Have a gravy drawn from the bones and trimmings, thickened with butter rolled in flour. Strain it into a small stew-pan, boil, and add a little lemon, pepper and salt.

RABBITS STEWED WITH ONIONS.—Clean a pair of nice rabbits; soak in cold salt water for an hour, to draw out the blood; put on in a large saucepan, with cold water enough to cover them, salt slightly, and stew until tender. Slice in another pot half a dozen onions, and boil in a very little water till thoroughly done. Drain off the water, stir into the onions a gill of drawn butter, pepper to taste, and when it simmers, add the juice of a lemon. Lay the rabbits in a hot dish, and pour over them the onion sauce. Let the dish stand in a warm place, closely covered, five minutes before serving.—*Common Sense in the Household.*

RECHAUFFE.—Cut slices of cold meat, put in a saucepan, and sprinkle over salt, pepper, and a handful of dry flour; cover with warm water, and add a piece of butter. Heat to boiling. A spoonful of catsup or curry may be added if wished.

BROILED SQUIRRELS.—Clean and soak to draw out the blood. Wipe dry, and broil over a hot, clear fire, turning often. When done, lay in a hot dish and anoint with melted butter, seasoned with pepper and salt. Use at least a teaspoonful for each squirrel, and let it lie between two hot dishes five minutes before serving.—*Marian Harland.*

TO BROIL YOUNG CHICKENS AND PIGEONS.—Pick, wash and dry the fowl. Cut down the back and truss, making it very flat, pepper and salt it. Place the inside on a gridiron previously heated, and put at a greater distance from the fire than for a steak. Take the gridiron off the fire occasionally, and rub the birds with butter, or butter liberally in dishing them.

"Broiling is the most delicate manual office of the cook, and requires the greatest facility, and most unremitting vigilance. You may turn your back on the stewpan or the spit, but the gridiron can never be left with impunity."

How to bake partridges. — Cut off the legs and wings at the second joints. Raise the body feathers with the fingers, and inlay with plenty of salt and pepper, then stroke back the feathers to their original position. Next knead your clay in water to the consistency of stiff paste, and plaster all over the bird till it resembles a huge dumpling. Then rake out a hollow in the hottest bed of coals, put in your dumplings, and cover carefully. When done break open carefully, and the birds appear divested of every particle of skin and feathers. The stomach and intestines will be shriveled to a hard ball, and by their retention will be found not to have impaired the flavor of the meat, but the rather to have imparted an additional relish. — *From the Fishing Tourist.*

Reed birds. — (*Henry Ward Beecher's receipt*). — Cut sweet potatoes lengthwise; scoop out of the center of each a place that will fit half the bird. Now put in the birds, after seasoning them with butter, pepper and salt, tying the two pieces of potato around each of them. Bake them. Serve them in the potatoes. Or they can be toasted or fried in boiling lard like other birds.

PANCAKES.—Stir one or two cupfuls of cream or milk into two beaten eggs; add flour or corn meal enough to make a thin batter. If the milk is sweet, add one teaspoonful of yeast powder; if it is sour, add instead of the yeast powder half a teaspoonful of soda, dissolved in a little warm water.—*Practical Cooking.*

MOTHER JOHNSON'S PANCAKES (ADIRONDACKS). — Enough flour is added to a quart of sour milk to make a rather thick batter. Let it stand *over night*, and in the morning add two well-beaten eggs with half a teaspoonful of soda, dissolved in a tablespoonful of warm water; bake at once.

RICE CAKES.— One cup of cold boiled rice; one pint of flour; one teaspoonful of salt; two eggs beaten light ; milk sufficient to make a tolerably thick batter.

CHOCOLATE. — Into one pint of boiling milk and water (equal quantities) put two squares of chocolate scraped fine ; boil five minutes or more, stirring frequently.

MANSFIELD CAMP BISCUIT.— Take one quart of "prepared flour" to one dozen biscuits. Mix with water into a dough, stirring with a spoon. When sufficiently stiff, turn it out on a board, and roll it with a long bottle, or can, to a half an inch in thickness. Cut out biscuits with a cup or the lid of a can. Sprinkle dry flour on the board, the bottle, and the biscuit cutter before using, to keep the dough from sticking. Put enough lard in a spider to cover the bottom; when hot, fry the biscuit brown in from five to ten minutes; turn them two or three times till well cooked through. Serve hot.

GEORGIA HOE CAKE.—Mix corn meal with lukewarm water to the consistency of a stiff dough; make into small round cakes about an inch thick. Use a hot bed of coals raked from the fire, and bake in a heavy iron frying-pan. Put an old tin plate over the pan, and cover with live coals. Cook quick and serve hot. Grease the pan before using, or which will answer the same purpose, sprinkle the bottom with dry meal. If the dry meal scorches as soon as it touches the bottom the pan is too hot.

HOE CAKE.—Make and bake as above, except use scalding water or milk, and after mixing let it stand an hour before baking.

MACARONI WITH CHEESE (*London Cooking School*)—Do not wash the macaroni; throw it, broken into convenient pieces, into boiling water which is well salted; stir or shake it frequently, to prevent its adhering to the bottom of the stewpan. The moment it is quite tender (no longer), pour it into a colander, and shake off all the water. In the meantime melt a lump of butter the size of a large egg (two ounces), to half a pound of macaroni, in a cup, and grate a handful (four ounces) of cheese. When the macaroni is well drained place a little in the bottom of the dish in which it is to be served ; pour over it some of the melted butter, and sprinkle over that a little grated cheese. Continue alternate layers of the three ingredients until all the macaroni is used, leaving butter and cheese on the top. Then bake it in the dish three or four minutes, or long enough for the macaroni to soak the butter and cheese; then take it out; brown the top with a hot kitchen shovel, and it will be ready to serve. Serve immediately. It requires about twenty-five minutes to boil macaroni.

MACARONI WITH TOMATO SAUCE.— Put butter, size of an egg, into a saucepan ; when it is at the boiling point throw in an onion (minced), two sprigs of parsley, chopped fine, and a little pepper. Let it cook five or eight minutes longer. Now pour in a coffee cup of tomatoes which have been stewed, and strained through a colander ; stir all together. Boil your macaroni in salt water until tender ; put in a layer of macaroni in a baking dish, pour over sauce, and again macaroni, and have sauce on top ; set in a moderate oven for three minutes. Serve immediately.

MASHED POTATOES.— Pare, and boil with salt in the water, until tender — then turn off the water ; put in a small lump of butter and a little milk, and mash fine.

Then serve. What is left from that meal you can make into potato balls, by mixing the yolk of an egg and a little flour with it, and then form into balls in a large spoon, with a knife. Fry them in good drippings until they are brown.

OMELETTE.— Take six eggs. Beat the whites very stiff; beat yolks separately, add to them salt and pepper, and a cup of milk, and then stir in the whites. Put a piece of butter in a frying-pan ; when it is hot, pour in the omelette. Cook about eight minutes, not letting it burn at the bottom. When done, lay a hot plate over the frying-pan, and turn the pan upside down, leaving the brown side of the omelette on top. All omelettes should be served instantly, or they will fall.

RICE OMELETTE.— Dissolve in one teacup of milk, one teacup of cold boiled rice ; mix in one tablespoonful of butter, a little salt, and then stir in three well beaten eggs; and bake as a plain omelette.— *Miss Tyson in The Queen of the Kitchen.*

MEAT OMELEITE.— Make an ordinary omelette; when done, before removing from the pan, spread minced ham thickly over the surface. Slip a knife under one edge of the omelette, and double it over on to the upper side ; then slip the knife under the opposite edge, and double that over, letting the edges lap considerably, so as to entirely inclose the meat.

64

GREAT NORTHERN PIKE (*Esox lucioides*).

CHAPTER VII.

ROD AND LINE.

IT is a curious fact that the first to publish a printed book on angling was a woman, Dame Juliana Berners. "This lady wrote that curious production 'The Boke of St. Alban's, which was imprinted at Westminster by Wynkin de Worde, the assistant and friend of Caxton.' This 'Boke' was published originally without 'The Treatyse of Fysshing,' which was added to it in 1496. Dame Juliana, who was eminent for piety and learning, and whose name ought to be held in veneration by anglers in all ages, was prioress of the nunnery of St. Sopwell near St. Albans, Hertfordshire." The lady must have been a sturdy dame, for she was accustomed to use a rod at least fourteen feet long. It was composed of three pieces, the joints of which were bound together by long hoops of iron. The butt was "a fayre staff of a fadom and a halfe longe and arme grate," that is, the size of one's arm. "The whole making a weight," says Fitzgibbon, "far too ponderous for the muscles of us modern males."

For the best fishing rod consult the authorities ; and after some experience you will find "the best rod is like the woman you live with,—you must find one that suits you best."

The rod must possess toughness, elasticity and lightness. It should also be adapted to its owner. We have elsewhere spoken of the stocking of a gun which ought to be in accordance with the general build and proportions of the shoulders, arms and neck of the sportsman using it. So the rod should be one that you can handle with ease and dexterity. For though the one weapon is vastly greater in weight than the other, yet for the one we use both hands and arms, while with the other, the weight and strain falls principally upon the fingers and wrist of one hand. For rods consisting of one piece, the ordinary cane fishing pole is the best. They are, however, difficult to carry, and unless you use a jointed rod, suitable material for poles had better be cut at the camp. Jointed rods are generally made of different kinds of wood. Lancewood has almost universally been used for tips and second pieces, while the butt is made of some hard but lighter wood, though recently bamboo is, by being carefully selected and finely wound with silk about the joints, considered quite as desirable, and in many instances preferred, on account of its lightness and elasticity, for tips and second joint, and also for the butt; and taking all things into consideration, the jointed bamboo rod is, for general fishing, more desirable than a wood rod.

The most perfect fly-rod is that known as the split bamboo. There are several makers of these rods whose methods of manufacture differ somewhat. A ten-foot bamboo rod weighs about ten ounces, and should be used with a reel weighing from 2 to $2\frac{1}{4}$ ounces.

Select a jointed rod of medium length and weight. The lightest rod is used for trout fishing; for black bass, a somewhat heavier and stiffer rod is used. Dr. J. A. Henshall, in his new and excellent " Book of the Black Bass," which contains much valuable and practical advice to the angler, says: "As a long, withy, willowy rod is best for casting a fly, so a short, stiffish rod is best for casting a minnow." In selecting a rod, the character of the waters to be fished in, and the kind of game to be fished for, must also be taken into consideration. For general fishing in all kinds of waters, a good jointed wood rod is the best. Dr. Henshall describes a black bass rod made by himself, composed of white ash for the first joint and lance-wood for the second joint and tip, eight feet and three inches in length, and weighing but eight ounces, with which he has killed many a black bass from two to four pounds in weight, and pickerel weighing from five to fifteen pounds; though to perform this feat with an eight ounce rod would be, for a novice, about as difficult as to make a cast of fifty yards.

General information in regard to fishing lines can be readily obtained. There are all kinds and varieties. Unless you are an expert, however, you had best commence with a limited supply. One or two medium-sized lines, and one good strong one, will probably answer your every purpose. For fly-fishing a twisted line is used. For trolling, and for casting with a minnow, a braided line is required, as twisted lines kink. For trout fishing, about one hundred feet of line is needed where there is plenty of room for play, and fifty feet of line is a good cast. The length of a trolling line should be from fifty to seventy-five yards.

Always dry your lines when possible, as soon as you are through with them. Waterproof lines can be easily obtained, but the following receipt for making the common fishing line water-proof may be of interest :

" Take of boiled oil two parts, and gold size one part; shake together in a bottle, and the mixture is ready for use. Apply to the line, thoroughly dried with a piece of flannel ; expose to the air, and dry. After using the line two or three times it should have another coat, the application being repeated when necessary.'

Gimp is a kind of twist with a metallic wire running through or around it, and is almost absolutely necessary for taking certain kinds of fish.

Silk-worm gut is the dried viscid fluid taken from the two lobes or sacs of the worm. Gut comes in short pieces about a foot in length, and of various qualities. Good gut is hard and can be tested by biting: "if it resists the teeth like wire, it is good."

A snell or snood is a very short light line to which the hook is fastened. It is generally made of gut. In fishing for pickerel or pike, gimp must be used on account of the numerous sharp teeth of these fish.

A leader is a short line generally composed of several lengths of gut tied together. The gut should be of different sizes, the largest for the rod end of the leader, and tapering gradually to the smallest size for the last length called the fly or hook end. The different lengths are tied either by a single or double water-knot, or by lapping the ends and tying a simple knot, as you would with a double string, cutting off the short ends close to the knot. The first two knots are slip-knots; and a dropper is easily put on by tying a knot at the end of the snell, then inserting the snell between the two pieces of gut before drawing the ties together. This is very convenient for changing droppers. With the last knot, the dropper is fastened by a half hitch just above the knot.

The becket-hitch is a secure knot for fastening the leader to the line and to the snell.

Gut should always be soaked before tying. Use

warm water. Gut comes both white and colored. Many color their own gut by soaking it in green tea, indigo, etc.

In regard to the color of snells and lines, remember that the fish is looking up through the water toward the sky, and therefore a colored gut, in clear water, which seems to you invisible, because you are looking toward the bottom of the stream, is to the trout perfectly plain and distinct.

For fly-fishing, the hook should be attached to a snell, and this to a leader, to which is fastened the line. And for all fishing except trolling it is best to use a snell. Take a small supply of snells and leaders with you. If you get out of leaders, make new ones from white horsehair. Let the leader lie in water a short time before casting.

Swivels are of great use in casting with a minnow, and one or two should always be used in trolling. They keep the line from kinking, and should be of brass.

In trolling, a spoon hook is used. There are many varieties, and one kind is about as good as another. Many prefer to have but one hook attached to the spoon, others use three hooks. Frequently a small tuft of bright-colored feathers is added. This is not of much value ; the principal thing is to have the spoon bright and not too large.

The "patent adjustable sinker," having a spiral

wire at each end, will be found very convenient, as it can be easily attached or detached from the line.

Do not, as a general thing, use a float.

Reels are of two kinds, the multiplying reel and the click reel. The first is used for bait fishing, the second for fly fishing. Some makers manufacture a combination reel which can be adapted to either method, and for the general fisher this is the best.

Casting is the proper method of letting the fly, or minnow, light upon the water. The reel should always be on the under side of the rod; and, for casting with a fly, below the hand, with a minnow, above the hand. With a fly, the first cast is made with a length of line about equal to that of your pole. The line is then gradually lengthened, a few feet at a time, with each subsequent cast, until you have as much out as you require.

It is somewhat difficult to learn how to cast, and is to be acquired more from practice than any information which can be given in books. There are hardly any two that perform the feat exactly alike. To cast with a minnow, the bait should be near the tip of the rod. Hold the rod in the right hand, and well to your right with the arm extended, then by a sharp quick motion bring the arm directly across the chest, allowing the line to freely unreel, and before the motion of the bait has stopped, by a strong swift stroke bring the rod from left to right, leaving the right arm extended straight from the shoulder, and the tip of the rod pointing a little this side the spot where the minnow is to fall. This cast is made with the rod all of the time *in front* of you.

To cast with a fly more length of line is required to commence with. Hold the rod in the right hand, and by a quick motion bring it up over the left shoulder. This will cause the fly to pass over your head to a considerable distance behind you, and just before it has reached its farthest point bring the rod forward with a strong, quick motion, leaving the arm extended, straight out, and the tip of the rod pointing directly toward the spot where the fly lights upon the water.

Striking is done by a dexterous turn of the wrist. Frequently a fish, in seizing a fly or bait, does not hook himself, and drops it; therefore to secure the fish, as soon as you feel the pull on the line, or the fish rises to the fly, you give a quick turn with the wrist (not a jerk), which causes the hook to fasten firmly. This is called striking.

Use from one to three flies. They should be about three feet apart. When you have three flies, the one nearest to you is called the hand-fly, or stretcher, the one at the end the tail-fly, and the center one is called the dropper. The hand fly is also called a dropper.

For fly fishing you require a good general assortment,

unless you are familiar with the district, and know just what to take.

Mr. Charles W. Stevens recommends for the Maine lakes the following flies :

1. Prouty,
2. Fiery Brown,
3. Blue Jay,
4. Grizzly King.
5. Tomah Joe,
6. Silver Doctor,
7. Scarlet Ibis,
8. Brown Hackle.

For land-locked salmon, "The most killing flies are yellow May-fly, the silver-gray with black head, the orange-brown hackle with black head and gray, and the yellow May-fly with turkey wing."

The following is Mr. W. H. H. Murray's advice for the Adirondack district: "In respect to 'flies,' do not overload your hook. Hackles, red, black and brown, six each. Let the flies be made on hooks from Nos. 3 to 1 Limerick size. All fancy flies discard. They are generally good for nothing, unless it be to show to your lady friends. In addition to the hackles, Canada fly (6) is an excellent fly ; green drake (6) ; red ibis (6) ; small salmon flies (6), best of all. If in the fall of the year, take English blue jay (6) ; gray drake (6), good."

"Wallace's Adirondacks" mentions as indispensable, the scarlet ibis, abbey, dark cinnamon, grizzly king and coachman. The following are also recommended : The professor, Montreal white miller, March brown, and hackles of various colors.

The hackles and duns of all colors, the English blue jay, the devil-fly, the alder, stone, May and sand flies, will generally be found good for all trout waters.

Mr. Pennell advocates the use of the following three "typical" hackles, excluding all other kinds of flies.

1. A dark green body; very dark green hackle for both legs and whisk.

2. A dark orange body; fiery or cinnamon brown hackle for legs and whisk.

3. A golden-yellow body; darkish golden olive hackle for legs and whisk.

Dr. Henshall says: "I have had more uniform success, day in and day out, with black, brown, red, yellow and grey hackles (palmers) than with winged flies."

Bass are caught with both fly and bait, or by trolling. The flies for bass should be a little larger and brighter than those for trout.

There are several kinds of perch that will rise to a fly, though as a general rule these fish take bait more readily.

Along toward dusk, and on bright moonlight nights, the white miller is very effective.

The kind of flies to be used varies greatly according to the season of the year, and the waters in which you fish. Often fish will rise on one day to a certain fly, and the next day you will be obliged to use a fly of an entirely different kind or color. The temperature of the air as compared to that of the water, whether the water be calm or ruffled by the wind, whether the day is bright or cloudy, and the time of fishing ; all have to be taken into consideration. Note what natural fly is upon the water, and select from your stock something as near like it as you have. Do not depend too much on this, for sometimes the fish will rise to that which has no resemblance to any winged thing on the face of the earth. Make up your stock mostly of plain and dark flies.

Pickerel rarely rise to a fly, and are trolled for with a spoon, or fished for with live bait, generally minnow. A very good and lasting bait, however, will be found by cutting a piece of pork rind into the shape of a small fish. The hook for pickerel fishing should always be on wire or gimp, as this fish has very sharp teeth.

There is much difference among the authorities as to whether one should fish up or down stream. The advocates of the former method argue with considerable force that, as the trout are headed up stream, you are less liable to be seen ; that when you strike from behind you are more liable to be successful, as the fish is moving from you, and that by this method you keep the water clear the whole length of your route ; whereas, if you come down stream you roil the water by wading, or with your boat. Those who prefer fishing down stream claim, among other reasons, that the bait continually floating down to your feet is a great annoyance, and that the nearer it comes to you the less your chances of a bite; also that by fishing up stream you can neither keep bait stationary nor are you able to guide it; and in rapid waters there is less noise, and the line is kept taut.

In wading the middle of the stream push along quietly. "Fish may not hear, but they can, like deaf people, feel concussion."

The science of baiting consists in knowing the habits of the fish you are after. Small fish require less bait than large ones. The common angle worm is always good for almost every kind of fish, and can often, if properly put on to the hook, be cast as successfully as the fly.

Worms can be taken from our cities and kept for weeks, if treated rightly. A most tempting bait, especially for a trout when he will not rise to a fly, is to take two or three good worms and hook them half an inch through the middle, leaving the ends dangling.

All bait should, as a rule, be kept in motion.

The author of "The Game Fish of the North" says: "Minnow is never properly baited unless it spins freely with every motion of the rod, and it must ever be kept moving. Of course the line must be armed with the swivel trace, and in baiting with dead minnows a Limerick hook should be used, under any other circumstances never. The dead minnow is preferable for rapid water. In ponds the minnow should be alive."

There are several ways of hooking minnows. Some pass the hook through the upper lip, some through both lips, and others place the hook in front of the dorsal fin, having the point covered by the skin, but not letting it penetrate the flesh. A recent correspondence in the "American Field," in relation to the proper way to hook minnows, has brought out a letter from an Iowa gentleman from which we quote: "Light tackle, composed of two hairs of gut, with a swivel in the center, and two No. 9 round bent hooks tied on the end back to back, makes up the most deadly tackle I have ever tried for still fishing with the live minnow; but for trout fishing I would discard the live minnow, and substitute the Scotch minnow tackle for fishing with the dead minnow. I would make it as follows: Unite two good stout hairs of gut in the center by means of a swivel; in knotting to the swivel tie down the ends of your gut with waxed silk. On one end make a loop for attaching to your line, on the other tie first one hook; above that tie another, facing the opposite way from your first; above your second tie a third facing the same way as your first, and above your third tie a fourth, facing the same way as your second; the whole to be distributed on the gut in such a way that the fourth hook will be distant from the first about the length of a medium sized minnow's body. In putting on your minnow put your fourth hook through his head, the second hook in the back behind the fin, and the first one in the tail, in such a manner that it is drawn up and twisted a little on one side. A minnow put on in such a fashion will revolve rapidly on being propelled through the water with slight jerks, and any one who acquires the knack of making the dead minnow spin, will forever discard the live minnow pail, and all the miseries attendant on carrying it through a hilly or densely wooded country. A small bag fastened to a buttonhole of the coat, and filled with a little wet moss constitutes the Scotch trout fisher's minnow carrier, and all who may ever try it, and succeed in putting on their minnow right, will find it the most deadly line they ever used."

Take with you a general but not too large assortment of fishing tackle. Your success in fishing is more likely to depend upon yourself than upon your tackle.

Fishing is an art, and keen indeed are the delights of the experienced sportsman, who with superior skill and implements enters into contest with the game fish of our country. But often you may camp where the fishing is considered poor; do not, however, despair of catching anything. Many a lake and pond which is considered fished out will readily furnish a supply for your camp, if you will only carefully examine it, and work properly, and in many a small clear stream which seems almost too insignificant to notice, trout will rise to your fly, perhaps the first fly that has ever been cast in those waters. Often very little reliance can be placed on the statements of those who reside in the neighborhood, who fish for only a few days in the year with poor tackle.

There is a tendency of late to so highly extol the exploits of the fly fisher, that one is led to forget that excellent sport can be had in pan fishing, which is less expensive, and at the same time requires no little skill and judgment. The habits of the pan fish, and the varieties of bait to be used, afford a wide field for study. Besides, a large number of the pan fish are most excellent eating, and if properly cooked make fully as choice a dish as many of the game fish.

In whatever waters you angle, take into consideration the habits of the fish you expect to take, what hours they feed, where their favorite haunts are, what kind of food they prefer, the conformation of the mouth, and the average size of the fish at that place. This is necessary, that you may know the size and kind of fly to be used, or the kind of bait necessary for your hook, and whether much or little is required.

The temperature of the water and the places where food can be found, cause bass and many other varieties of fish to change their locality, sometimes even from day to day.

As a rule, the morning and evening hours are the best. If you choose a morning hour you had better, if your fishing place be any great distance, carry a lunch with you, and take a late breakfast. A hastily prepared breakfast, and as hastily eaten, spoils many a good day ; besides, the chances are that you will almost always arrive at the fishing ground just a little too late. If you must have a warm breakfast first, then rise in time to have it cooked before daylight. To be at the right place at the right time is a matter of great importance.

CHAPTER VIII.

HOW TO MAKE A FISH NET AND HAMMOCK.

THE making of a net is a very simple matter. You require only a needle, a mesh-stick and the material for a net. The needle is made of a narrow, flat piece of wood cut in the shape shown in Fig. 1. On this needle the thread or twine is placed, but care should be taken not to lay on so much as to make the needle bulky or difficult to pass through the meshes. A new length of twine can easily be added. The mesh-stick may be round, square or flat, and from six inches to a foot in length. It must be borne in mind that the length of each mesh will be just twice the circumference of the mesh-stick. The length of the needle should be about the same as that of the mesh-stick.

Having laid sufficient length of twine upon the needle, unwind one or two feet and fasten the end, *A*, Fig. 1, firmly to a hook or nail in the wall. Next make a loop (the size of the mesh-stick) just below the hook. The loop hangs to the right (see dotted line *C*, Fig. 1). You are now ready to commence the net. Hold the needle in the right hand, take the mesh-stick in the left,

and bring the twine down over the mesh-stick held
just below the loop; pass the needle around under the
stick and up from below through the loop, then draw
down until the bottom of the loop rests upon the top

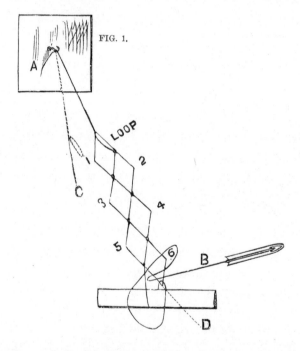

FIG. 1.

of the mesh-stick (see mesh 6, Fig. 1). Hold it in position with the left thumb while you throw the twine
over the left thumb and up over its own standing part
and across the loop; then bring the needle down under

the loop, and up between the loop and the standing part; pull evenly to the right, then downward toward the right, in the direction of dotted line *D*, Fig. 1, letting the knot fasten just above the bottom of the loop. Slip out the mesh-stick and repeat the same operation, except that you use the mesh just made instead of the loop. Keep on making in this way one mesh after another until you have a string of meshes as in Fig. 1, the length of which must be just twice the width of the net, exclusive of the loop, which is not a mesh, and therefore, must not be counted. Thus, if you have forty meshes, twenty meshes will measure the width of the net. Having completed the requisite number of meshes, unfasten from the hook and untie the loop, for it is not the right size for a mesh.

Now open your meshes evenly and you will find you have two rows, one above the other, like the first two rows of Fig. 2, and of the width of the net. Run a short piece of twine through the top row of meshes (Nos. 2, 4, 6, etc., Fig. 2), and tie the ends together. This forms a temporary cord upon which your work hangs, and which is now thrown over the hook; or if preferred, a long smooth stick can be passed through the first row of meshes and held in place by fastening with strings at each end.

The first two rows of meshes being completed and the proper width thus obtained, the required length of the net is obtained by simply adding a sufficient number of rows to the first two. Hang up the work by throwing the cord which holds it over the hook, letting the work hang on the side which brings the last mesh of the second row to the left, and, commencing with the last mesh of the second row, knot through it, using the mesh-stick and needle just as before. The new mesh will be the first one on the third row. Knot through the next mesh of the second row in the same way, and so on till the new row is completed ; making as many meshes as your stick will conveniently hold before slipping them off. Turn the work and add the fourth row, and thus keep on till you have the required length. Always turn the work after completing a row so that in making the next one, you commence at the left and knot toward the right. A square is the best shape for an ordinary net.

A hammock is made in the same way, with the addition of guys at each end to the body or bed of the hammock. The guys (Fig. 2) are long meshes at each end, knotted, like the smaller meshes, through the first and last row of the hammock. The twine is wound a number of times around the stick before knotting, in order to give the required length. Be careful to wind evenly, and always, except for the first guy, the same number of times round the stick. Three or four feet is about the proper length for a guy.

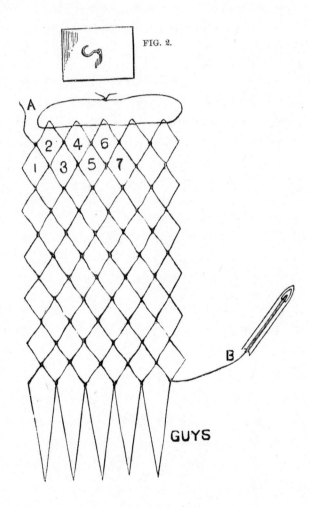

FIG. 2.

GUYS

The hammock is now complete with the exception of the end ropes for hanging. These should be of good stout rope and tied very securely. They may be fastened directly to the guys, or rings with curved edges, called thimbles, can be used. Whether thimbles are used or not, the end of the guys should be bound or "served," as it is called, to prevent friction. Lay the guys at each end evenly together, then slip a small rope through them all, and pull hard so as to stretch each guy its full length ; wind your rope evenly around the guys some four or five inches each way from the center, then bring the two sides of the guys together and bind them for an inch or two, thus making an "eye," through which passes your large rope for hanging.

Before commencing a net or hammock, it is best to experiment with a piece of common cotton twine until you learn the stitch. The needle and mesh-stick for this purpose can be cut out of a piece of pasteboard.

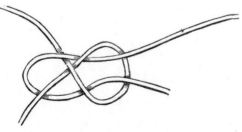

BECKET HITCH.

In fastening two pieces of twine together use the weaver's knot or becket-hitch.

A CANVAS HAMMOCK.

To make a canvas hammock, take for the body a piece of light duck, six feet six inches long, and of the widest width that comes. Make a wide hem at each end, and in each hem work eyelet-holes about three inches apart. Next make loops at each end of the cloth, as follows: Run one end of your twine through the first eyelet-hole, and fasten the end to the body part by a bowline knot, a few inches from the eyelet, thus making a small loop in which runs your eyelet-hole. Then pass all your twine, except the last eight feet, through the next eyelet-hole, and inclose the second eyelet by a small loop like the first. You will now have a long piece of twine between the two eyelet-holes, which makes a long loop, which should be just four feet in length. Make in the same way, between the second and third eyelet-holes, another long loop of exactly the same length as the last; and thus keep on to the last eyelet-hole. See that all of your loops, both large and small, are of exactly the same length, and cut off the surplus end of your twine.

The hammock is now complete, with the exception of the ropes for hanging. These ropes should be very strong, and are fastened, one at each end of the hammock, by placing the loops at each end evenly together, and running the end of a rope through all the *long* loops at that end, and tying by a bowline knot, or, if you know how to make a short splice, that is the nicest way to attach the rope to itself, after running it through the loops. It would perhaps be better to work the corner eyelets first, and then put in the others at equal distance from each other. If you make the hem at the ends wide enough, an extra seam just back of the eyelets can be run. This will form a long case, into which insert a stout stick or piece of cane-pole, to keep the hammock stretched open when hung. Sew up the ends tight, or the stick will slip through, owing to the weight of the body.

CHAPTER IX.

THE HORSE-HAIR FISH LINE.

ONE of the chief delights of the lover of out-of-door life is to be independent, and able to shift for himself. The real sportsman should know at least how every article he uses is made, if he cannot make it; and there is no small satisfaction in being your own manufacturer, whenever it is practicable. As a pure horse-hair line is not easily to be found in the market, and possesses many advantages, we give here full directions for making one. There is sometimes found a combined silk and hair line, but these lines have not proven satisfactory. Either use a pure silk or a pure hair line. The horse-hair line is very light, strong and durable. It will not rot like the silk line. Frequently it will be found that it can be used effectually where other lines have failed to show a single nibble. If you wish a line light in color, and almost transparent, use white hairs only, and with age the line will improve in tone. A dark line to resemble the fine roots and dead grasses always to be found in streams, should be made of reddish or brown hair, with a few black hairs interwoven. Remember it is a *horse*-hair line. Use hairs from the tail of a horse only, not from a mare. The latter are too weak and brittle. The size of a line depends upon the use it is to be put to, the rule is, one hair will sustain a pound of dead weight; but allowance must be made for sudden strains or jerks, and therefore extra hairs are required. A fine trout line can be made from nine hairs, and will be strong enough for all ordinary fishing.

Before commencing your line, wash the hair in tepid water, using a little soap. This not only cleans the hair, but makes it softer and more pliable. Next dry thoroughly, and see that the hairs lie nicely together. Then fold them in a newspaper, leaving the large ends out a trifle, so as to be easily picked up.

There are three ways of making a horse-hair line:

1. Take three spools of ordinary size. Whittle off one end of each, leaving the end slightly tapering, but not so thin as to split too easily. Cut three round smooth pegs that fit nicely into the holes of the spools, leaving one end of the peg square, and larger than the round part, so as to form a head which can be easily taken hold of. The whole peg is about half an inch long. For a trout line take nine hairs, which may be of unequal length, but for a first experiment had better be pretty long. Lay the large or coarse ends evenly together, and tie a knot at the extreme end. Tie

another knot half an inch below the first. You require a good steady purchase, and for this purpose attach your hair, between the two knots, to a hook or nail driven into a tree or your tent pole. Divide your hair into three strands, running each strand through one of the spools, so that the small end of the spool will be toward the knots. Slip your spools up within a couple of inches of the second knot, and insert your pegs tightly at either end of the spool to keep the hairs in their place, and to prevent the spool from slipping. Hold the line, which remains attached to the hook, between the thumb and forefinger of the left hand. Take up one of the spools with the *right* hand, and twist the strand toward the right. Then lay it *over* the other strands, and hold it in position by placing it under the left thumb. Take another spool, twist in the same way, always to the right. Lay that strand over the other two, holding the two last in position with the thumb. Repeat the same thing with the last spool.

You now have the three spools in position. To avoid confusion mark them 1, 2 and 3, commencing with the right hand spool. Take up the right hand spool, No. 1, letting the next one, No. 2, drop; it will take care of itself. Give the strand two or three turns, and lay it over strand No. 3, which is still held in position between the left forefinger and thumb.

93

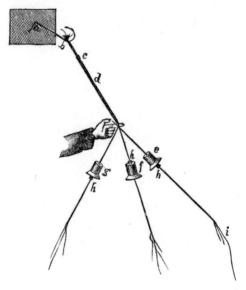

a, hook; b, first knot; c, second knot; d, main strand, or line; e, f, g, spools Nos. 1, 2, and 3; h, h, h, pegs; i, added hair, with end projecting a little above the forefinger.

Hold it there and pick up spool No. 2, letting No. 3 drop, and give it two or three twists and lay the strand over No. 1, holding it there. Pick up No. 3 and repeat the same thing, and thus go on. In a few moments you will see the beginning of a neat round line, one of the most finished lines you ever handled, providing you have done your work right. The operation is very simple. Twist *always to the right*, and lay *over* to the left.

Loosen your pegs and slip down your spools as occasion requires, but do not allow too much distance between your spools and the line you are making. The shorter the distance the tighter and more compact your line will be. There is such a thing, however, as making it too compact and unyielding. Do not twist so much as to kink your strands. A little practice and your own judgment will enable you to know what is required. The line can be made of any length, and only careful inspection will show where the hairs join.

To add a fresh hair you have merely to take out the peg and run the coarse or large end of the hair through the spool close along the strand, and about half an inch beyond the main strand or line. Insert the peg. Place the fresh hair under the line just where the three strands unite ; it is held in place by thus being between the line and the left forefinger. Now give the spool several turns, and go on as before. As a rule you need pay no attention to the end of the hair just running out. It will shortly work itself to one side. Always add the fresh hairs to the strand that is to be laid over next. To prevent confusion, and to preserve even thickness of line, do not add two or three hairs all at once, and for this reason the hairs should be of unequal length. When your line is completed you will have a large number of short ends sticking out on all sides. Fasten your line to something firm above you and suspend by it a slight weight so as to stretch the line a little, but not strain it. Take a sharp knife and neatly cut off the ends close to the line. You can cut on the thumb nail. Use the greatest of care to avoid injuring the line itself.

The diagram upon the opposite page is sufficient to explain how this line is made:

In the place of spools small sticks can be used. Take a green branch about as large around as the forefinger. Cut three pieces from it from five to six inches long. Split them half way up with your knife, and insert your hairs in the split. Work these sticks the same way you would the spools.

2. A second method of making a line is to proceed exactly in the way last described, except that instead of laying the strands over each other, you simply make the ordinary three-strand plait. This will give you instead of a round line a flat line. It looks well, is

serviceable, and can be made much quicker, but is by no means equal in strength or finish to the other.

3. Another method is as follows : To make a line, say of eight hairs, pull out from your paper the required number. See that they are of about equal length and have them all run the same way, that is the larger ends, or roots, all together.

Place the large ends together, and tie a single knot at the extreme end of the strand. Now tie another knot half an inch lower down. Separate your eight hairs into two strands of four hairs each, and tie a knot at the end of each strand. Next cut from the neighboring bush (for we will suppose you are in camp waiting for the rain to stop) two small forked twigs. Trim them, and cut off from each, one of the branches about half an inch from the fork, and cut the other branch four or five inches above the fork. You now have two small hooks with the shank about five inches in length. Insert your hooks or twigs, one in each strand of your line, just under the knots at the ends. You must have a weight at the other end, and you will probably find your pocket knife the most convenient article at hand. Open the large blade part way, fold a piece of paper over the edge to prevent its cutting the hair, and then close it down upon the line between the first and second knots. Pick up your twigs, one in each hand, and turn them slowly with the fingers, being careful that you turn them in opposite directions, say the right hand one from you, the left hand one toward you. Raise the arms so as to let the knife be suspended in the air, and its weight will keep the strands straight. In a moment the knife will commence to revolve, and your separate strands will twist together. By holding the twigs or hooks well apart, the line will be more compact. When finished take off your twigs and make another piece in the same way. Tie the pieces together by a neat, strong knot, and thus keep on to any desired length.

This is the most expeditious way of making a horse-hair line, but it is somewhat objectionable on account of the number of knots, which, especially with a reel, would be inconvenient.

The following diagram explains the whole process.

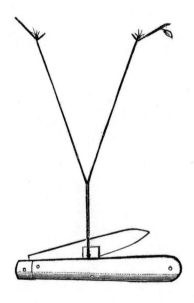

CHAPTER X.

THE GUN.

IF you are not going specially for hunting do not carry too many guns nor too much ammunition. Unless the hunting is exceedingly good, a couple of shot guns and a rifle will answer for quite a number. Ascertain, as far as possible, the kind and quantity of game in the district you expect to visit, and as most districts are greatly overrated, due allowance must be made for this.

In purchasing a sporting arm, if you have not already had some experience in hunting, it is best to advise with some experienced friend. Many young men think that their first gun must be the latest and most expensive article in the market. This is a mistake. Buy something good but not the most expensive, and after you have become something of a sportsman, you will be better able to judge for yourself just what you want.

Unless you expect to hunt for large game always, you will have far more use for a shot gun than for a rifle ; and remember, that whatever you buy, the difference of a few ounces in weight on a long day's tramp is a matter of considerable importance.

Breech-loaders, on the whole, are preferable ; however, do not despise the old-fashioned muzzle-loader. The author of "Gun, Rod and Saddle" says : "Cartridges are troublesome and bulky to carry, and if the stock should run short, a considerable loss of time might elapse before a fresh supply could be obtained, but there is no place from a trading-post to a hamlet where the ordinary loose ammunition cannot be obtained."

Mr. Joseph W. Long, the author of that admirable work, "American Wild Fowl Shooting," also says : "The chief superiority of the breech-loader lies in its capability of being so quickly reloaded when in the field or boat, and this alone is a sufficient advantage to compensate for many otherwise serious objections. This one requirement, however, being often wanting, the advantage is not conclusive. On pleasant days, when shooting from my boat, I usually made a practice of reloading as fast as possible between shots, carrying an ammunition box and loading tools with me for that purpose ; but this, for obvious reasons, I could not well do on stormy days, or when shooting away from my boat, and consequently I had to refill my shells at night—often when I should be sleeping—or else forego my morning shooting next day."

For rapidity of firing there is no question that the breech-loader is the most desirable; it is more easily loaded, is much safer than the muzzle-loader, and can now be had at reasonable prices. Taking all things into consideration it is best if you intend purchasing a sporting arm to select a breach-loader. In selecting do not overlook the new hammerless guns.

In purchasing, attention should be paid to the stocking of the gun. As a rule, "a sportsman having short arms and a short neck requires a straight stocked gun, and *vice versa*." You should take into consideration the proportions of your figure, especially the arms, neck and shoulder.

Accustom yourself to a certain amount of pressure in pulling the trigger, and as far as possible always retain the same.

Keep your gun in good order; the better care you give it, the better service it will do you. Guns used on salt water require special attention. Do not use vegetable oil for the locks, nor any oil not free from salt. Before starting it is advisable to go to a gunsmith and have your gun examined; also have him show you how to take the lock to pieces, and how to put it together again.

You cannot expect to shoot well unless you thoroughly understand your gun. To do this, you should practice with a target until you know the range of your gun, the amount of ammunition required, whether it shoots high or low, etc. Practice carefully, take notes, and pay attention to every little detail.

Do not use too much shot. The more lead you use, the greater the friction and resistance to the force of the explosion.

Mr. Long says: "As to the amount of shot used for duck shooting, from my own experience and observation of the charges used by the most successful duck hunters of my acquaintance, I find the best proportions to be: For a 10-gauge, 4 to $5\frac{1}{2}$ drams of powder, 1 and $1\frac{1}{4}$ ounces shot; for a 9-gauge, $4\frac{1}{2}$ to 6 drams powder, 1 to $1\frac{3}{8}$ ounces shot; for an 8-gauge, 5 to 7 drams powder, $1\frac{1}{8}$ to $1\frac{1}{2}$ ounces shot."

In cleaning a muzzle-loader be thorough, but expeditious. Wipe out the barrels as well as you can, then wind a piece of cloth around your cleaning rod so that it fits snugly in the barrel. Force the rod rapidly up and down with the hammers up. The air thus quickly drawn in and expelled, will soon dry the gun. Care should be taken to wrap your cloth so that no small pieces or threads will remain in the gun, as they are apt to ignite upon the first discharge, and, remaining in the barrel still burning, might, if the gun were immediately reloaded, cause a serious accident.

With a double-barrelled gun do not accustom yourself to fire too much from one barrel. It is better for your gun and for yourself that you use them about equally.

In aiming, where the object is near and stationary, your eye should run along the barrel, the sight on a line with the object; but if the object be some distance and moving, then due allowance must be made for *distance, direction, and rapidity of motion*, and the aim must be sufficiently in advance and above the object, in order to kill. When the object is moving rapidly, calculation must be made as to the amount of space it will pass over during the time the lead is traveling toward the object, *i. e.* in order to cause two moving bodies to meet at a certain angle, you must know at what rate of speed each travels. The space gained between the moment of pulling the trigger and the arrival of the shot varies greatly with different birds. For instance, in shooting at a flying fowl, the following elements enter into a successful shot: The laws of flight, the direction the fowl is taking, the force and direction of the wind as affecting its flight, the distance of the fowl from you, the distance your gun will carry, the laws of gravitation and deflection as affecting your charge, judgment as to the point where the charge and fowl will meet, the correctness of your aim toward that point, the steady motion of your gun in case such motion is required, your ability to discharge your gun at the precise moment of correct aim, and the reliability of your gun for execution.

The direction of the object from you, whether it be stationary, straight ahead and rising, directly above, or crossing to the right or left, will cause a difference in your aim.

We quote again from " American Wild Fowl Shooting."

" Never bring up the gun in a direction opposite to the bird's flight, nor put it up in any way in front of the birds, waiting for them to come to it ; but wait until they get nearly to you, and then, bringing the gun up directly behind them, carry it forward quickly in the exact line of their flight, and pull the trigger without stopping the motion of the gun. The precise time of pulling and the amount of space which must be allowed in front of them and behind the line of aim, will, of course, vary greatly in accordance with the direction and apparent velocity of their flight, and the probable distance they may be from the shooter. All these conditions, and the allowance to be made, you must estimate almost instantly, whilst putting up the gun, and without musing or pondering over it. This, of course, can be learned only by practice ; no instruction can convey the art. * * * To kill mallard when flying at their usual rate of speed, I myself should aim, I think, about two feet, or their length, in advance, if at a distance of thirty-five yards from them. This may help to give the tyro a proximate idea of it, though he may find in practice, for the reasons given above, his proper allowance to be either a little more or less. * * * Do not use shot of too large size, nor try to get too near, but give your charge a chance to spread. * * * In shooting over your cripples, which should be done as soon as possible, secure the liveliest one first, and try if you can get two or three in a line, to shoot them before they separate. The dead ones should be the last gathered."

When firing into a flock or covey aim at the farthest birds first.

Learn to fire at the moment of obtaining correct aim, and if it be at running or flying game, do not stop the motion of your gun when you pull the trigger.

Always take aim, and aim at some one thing. It is frequently remarked that with certain shots no aim is required. This we think is a mistake. There is often on the part of good sportsmen an unconscious aim, combined with good judgment and a nicety of calcula- tion. Aim is required, but the sights are only to *assist* in aiming, not to be used in every instance. Sometimes your aim will be directly over the top of your barrels, so as to cover the bird with them ; in such case the ends of your barrels are of as much or more assistance than the sight.

It must be constantly borne in mind, that the charge is affected by the law of gravitation, and if the range be long, and the aim be directly toward the center, the charge will fall considerably below; also the rules for aiming with the rifle are somewhat different from those of a shot gun. A little practice, and a few hints from an old sportsman, both in regard to your gun and rifle, will teach you far more than you can learn in books.

In carrying a gun always keep the muzzle well elevated. Never throw the stock behind the shoulder with the muzzle in front of you, nor hold the stock under the arm, with the muzzle pointing to the ground. By the first method, if you trip, the stock is thrown forward, the hammers striking the ground are very apt to cause a discharge of the gun; numerous are the fatal accidents caused in this way. By the second method, if the muzzle of the gun becomes clogged with snow or clay, as is likely to happen in going up hill or in leaping a ditch, the gun is apt to burst at the next discharge. It is well known that you can burst a gun by discharging it with the muzzle held even a few inches under water. Therefore in taking a gun from another person, look and see that the muzzle is free and open.

Carry a loaded gun always at half cock, never with the hammers down.

CHAPTER XI.

BOATS AND BOATING.

FOR the average camper, a small row-boat, capable of holding from two to three persons, and one with which a sail can be used, if required, is the best. In selecting a boat, consider safety and comfort, rather than lightness and speed. All canoes require great care and presence of mind in handling, and should not be used by children or inexperienced persons. Unless it is desired to take an extended trip by water, or you are an experienced boatman, and prefer your own craft, it is not advisable to take any boat. Boats adapted to the district can be found at almost all camping grounds; and where guides are used, it will generally be found that they get along better with the kind of boats to which they are accustomed. If you take a boat with you, see that it is adapted to the district which you intend to visit. A light twenty-pound canoe or canvas boat, which is suitable for going up a trout stream, or paddling down a river, may be the means of causing your death within thirty minutes after sailing into an inland lake, which is liable perhaps at any moment to be tossed by a squall. In rowing, paddling, or sailing, it must always be borne in mind that small lakes, especially in mountainous districts, are liable to sudden squalls. If you see a squall coming, make for shore if possible. If this cannot be done, lower sail and head the boat directly toward the wind, and keep her steady in that position. If your boat capsizes, do not get excited : presence of mind and perfect control are absolutely essential the first two minutes. Cling to your boat till you have time to collect your thoughts and determine what is the best course to pursue.

In sailing never belay the sheet, nor lower sail in a strong wind without first heading the bow in the direction of the wind.

In the matter of selecting a boat, it is almost impossible, and hardly within the compass of this book, to give advice, as everything depends upon the taste and requirements of the purchaser. The point to be considered is, what do you expect of your boat ? There are many kinds of boats manufactured and possessing excellent qualities, but each kind is generally adapted to a special purpose.

Canvas boats will not stand much sea, and cannot be used without injury in rivers filled with boulders and snags, but for smooth water they are very good, and have the advantage of being packed in a small compass. A canvas boat can easily be made by any one having a little skill. They are, however, as a rule, not much lighter than a good canoe, and, of course, if the canvas becomes wet through lack of proper water-proofing, considerable weight is added to the boat.

CHAPTER XII.

NIGHT SPEARING.

THE outfit necessary for a night's spearing is a boat, a jack, spears, and good warm clothing, including rubber boots. Too great precaution cannot be taken against dampness and cold.

A large flat-bottomed skow with square ends is the best boat for this purpose, as it draws but little water, and two persons can stand at the bow.

The spear-head should be of steel, with from four to six tines, and the shank enlarged gradually, forming a socket for the insertion of the pole. The pole, or handle of the spear, must be joined neatly to the head to prevent needless noise when thrust into the water, and should be round, smooth, and about ten feet in length and one and three-eighths inches in diameter.

The jack is an apparatus consisting of wire or bands of metal for holding such inflammable material as is used for a light. It is fastened to the bow of the boat, directly in the center, and should extend about three feet beyond the bow over the water.

The "basket-jack" can be used with pine knots, hickory bark, and pieces of pitch pine or well dried poplar.

A very serviceable and inexpensive jack, made to burn kerosene, can be easily constructed in the following manner : A tank or reservoir of heavy tin or galvanized iron, which will hold about two quarts, is placed upon a strong pole, or rest, in the bow of the boat, and about four feet from the bottom. From the lower part of the reservoir extends an iron tube (gas pipe will answer) $3\frac{1}{2}$ feet in length by $\frac{3}{8}$ inches in diameter. This tube has a stop-cock placed an inch or two from the reservoir. At the other end of the tube, which extends beyond the bow, two short pieces of hoop-iron are riveted at each end. These two hoops cross each other at right angles, and are bent so as to form a sort of hollow ball. This ball is for the purpose of holding and sustaining a ball of cotton or candle wicking, which is wound tightly round the end of the tube, which should be exactly in the center of the ball. If you have not sufficient wicking, old rags will do for a foundation. A piece of copper wire should be wound at intervals round the wicking to make it firmer.

Turn on the oil and thoroughly saturate the ball with kerosene ; then it is ready to light. The supply of oil should be so regulated by the stop-cock as to keep the wicking well saturated but without dripping.

A dark night is preferable for this sport. There must be no wind, as little or nothing can be accomplished when there are ripples on the water. Have one man to propel the boat. Use a pole instead of oars and handle it as quietly as possible. Unless the water be very clear, do not go where it is over four or five feet deep.

In spearing, allow for the laws of refraction. Also remember that the boat is in motion, and perhaps the fish. Your aim should be, not directly at, but a proper distance this side of, the fish.

Pickerel are found in still water among pond lilies and other aquatic plants, and around old submerged stumps, logs and sticks. Red-horse, Buffalo and Suckers are found early in the evening in the warm shallow water along the edges of lakes and rivers, and in the little bayous and marshes; but toward the latter part of the night they seek deeper water. Black Bass generally frequent deep water at night, and consequently few are taken in this way.

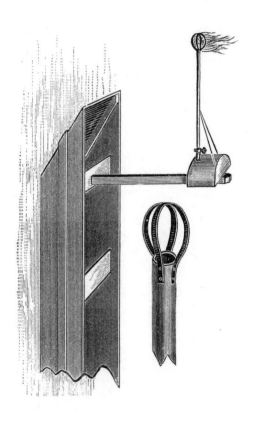

CHAPTER XIII.

ACCIDENTS AND AILMENTS.

[For the following valuable information to the camper, the author is indebted to Dr. E. Andrews, of Chicago, whose reputation as a surgeon is too widely known to need any added word of praise.]

DISLOCATIONS.

ONE of the most frequent dislocations is that of the shoulder. There are several ways of discovering this dislocation. One of the best signs is that of a hollow immediately below the projecting point of the shoulder blade. By pressing the fingers against the sound shoulder you will notice that immediately below the top of the shoulder blade, where the arm joins the shoulder, it feels firm and hard ; now, if, on testing the injured shoulder, you find a depression or hollow at this spot, you may know the shoulder is dislocated or broken. Another way of determining is to take the hand of the injured arm, and clasp it over the top of the sound shoulder. The elbow will stick out straight forward, and if it takes great force to press the elbow down, it is a sign that the shoulder is dislocated. To set the limb, lay the patient on the ground with the injured arm stretched out at right angles to his body. Take off your boots, and sit on the ground opposite the dislocated shoulder, and facing it. Take hold of the arm with both hands, and put one foot against the patient's side, and as close up under the arm as possible. Place the ball, or base of the great toe of the other foot against the prominence of the shoulder blade, but not too far down. Then pull slowly upon the arm, and push with the feet. Generally by steady pulling, and working the arm to and fro, it will slip into its place with a jerk. If necessary, some one can assist you in pulling.

Dislocations of the elbow are less frequent, and more difficult to distinguish from a fracture. When they occur, most of them can be set by taking hold of the wrist, and making a tolerably strong pull in the direction with the limb. If this does not restore the elbow to its proper position, it will be necessary to go to the nearest doctor.

Dislocations of the hip and knee are difficult for those not familiar with them to understand, and the best way is for the patient to obtain professional assistance as soon as possible.

Dislocations of the ankle are in four directions. 1. Where the foot is simply turned over in the joint, so that the sole is bent either inward or outward. Either of these dislocations is easily set by pulling the foot around into its place. 2. Where the foot either slips backward, leaving the heel sticking out behind, or slips forward, leaving the heel too short behind. These can be set by the patient lying on his back, and bending the limb so that the thigh points straight upward and the leg below the knee is horizontal. One person passes a towel under the knee, and another person takes hold of the foot. These two pull against each other. Let a third person take the foot in one hand, and the ankle in the other, and push the foot into its place. The dislocation of the foot backward is exceedingly prone to slip out again after being set. If it will not stay, the patient must start for home.

FRACTURES.

A fracture is a break. When a bone is broken, an examination will usually show that the limb is bent in some place where it should be straight and firm, and a grating sensation will be easily noticed by the hand of a person rubbing the broken surfaces of the bone together. When a bone breaks at a joint, it is often difficult to distinguish it from a dislocation, and care should be taken to ascertain which it is. A broken bone will generally unite in about six weeks. It is desirable to put the parts together as·soon as possible, but no great harm will happen if several days should elapse before it is done. To set a broken limb, you first put the bones in a proper position, and then apply immediately splints and bandages to hold them there. In most instances if you take hold of the hand or foot of the broken limb, and make a slow, steady, moderately firm pull, the bone will come into place of itself. The next thing is to hold the parts in position.

If it be a broken leg, a good plan is to take a blanket and fold it lengthwise till the width is equal to the length of the limb. Lay the broken limb across the center of the folded blanket, still keeping the leg pulled pretty firmly. Let two persons station themselves one at each end of the blanket, and commence to roll the ends tightly toward the leg until each roll comes in contact with its own side of the limb extending from the foot to the hip. Then take strips of cloth and pass them around the whole at intervals of about six inches, binding the rolls snugly against the leg. This is called a blanket splint. Sometimes a piece of board is placed on the outer side of each roll. If caught away from where a blanket can be procured, make splints of long firm strips of bark cut from a basswood or other tree. The strips should be about the size of the broken leg, and should be lined with pieces of cloth before being bound on to each side of the limb.

Where an arm is broken above the elbow, one of the

best splints is to peel some strips of bark about the size of the broken limb. Bind the bark all around the arm and support it by a sling around the neck. If the arm be broken below the elbow, get two flat pieces of wood as wide as the hand, and long enough to go from the tips of the fingers to the elbow. Pad with old towels, pieces of torn cloth, moss, or leaves, and place one piece of wood on the front, and the other piece on the back of the forearm, and bandage snugly and put in a sling.

Be careful in bandaging not to draw so tightly as to stop the circulation of the blood.

After a fracture or dislocation, a person should abandon, if possible, the trip, and go home, as the nature of the accident may not be thoroughly understood, and serious consequences might follow.

WOUNDS.

Gun-shot wounds are dangerous or not, according to their size and the nature of the parts injured. If a bone is broken by a ball, treat like other fractures with this difference, that the bandaging should be so arranged as to allow the dressing of the wound without taking off the splints.

Bullet wounds which do not fracture a bone or injure an important organ, are not very dangerous, and may be dressed with a simple wet cloth, bound on with a bandage, or handkerchief. It is desirable to extract the bullet, if possible, but if it cannot be found, no great anxiety need be felt.

Bullet wounds rarely bleed much. Wounds made with sharp instruments bleed pretty freely at first, but if no large vessels are cut, the blood soon stops flowing.

There are many ways of treating wounds, and each wound has to be treated according to its special character. It would therefore be impossible to give direction in detail, but the following rules will be found serviceable to the camper :

1. Flesh wounds made by a sharp instrument, which do not bleed much, and have not injured internal organs, should be bandaged carefully so as to keep the edges of the wound close together. This is the most favorable method for their healing.

2. If a wound bleeds copiously, and the bleeding will not stop by firmly pressing on the wounded part, open the wound wide, wipe it out boldly, and see exactly what spot the blood comes from ; then press the fingers firmly upon that spot, which is most generally to be found on the side next to the body.

The flowing of blood can often be held back for hours in this way by the wounded party himself, or by some other person holding his finger on the right place. Often this will be sufficient in itself to stay the flowing of the blood after a little while, owing to clots of blood forming in the end of the vessel under the finger.

3. If a man is cool and collected he can often pick up the artery or vein from which the blood flows, by seizing hold of it with a pair of tweezers, or the sharp point of a corkscrew, or a piece of bent wire. Pull the vessel out a little, and tie it with a strong thread or small string. To do this you must open the wound, and seek boldly for the cut vein or artery.

4. If the bleeding is obstinate it can generally be stopped by filling the wound with a towel, or handkerchief, or a sponge wrapped in cloth, and firmly pressed in. You can hold the pad in place by a rather tight bandage, or with the hand.

5. Bleeding in a wounded limb can almost always be stopped by tying a handkerchief loosely on the side of the wound next to the body; then put a stick under the handkerchief, and keep turning it around until the handkerchief is twisted very tightly. This will stop the blood entirely from flowing into the limb. This method is effectual, but it must be remembered it is only for temporary purposes, till assistance can be procured. If persisted in over sixty minutes mortification of the limb is liable to set in. Often blood stopped in this way forms clots at the mouth of the wound, which will prevent a renewal of the bleeding when the bandage is untwisted. For this reason it is better to un-

twist slowly, so as not to cause a too sudden rush of blood into the wound.

Wounds opening the cavities of large joints, especially the knee, are apt to give rise to a very dangerous inflammation. If such an accident occurs it is best to close the wound instantly, and keep it carefully and tightly shut. In this way the joint sometimes heals without trouble, but there is serious danger, and the camper who has opened a large joint should be carried to a surgeon as quickly as possible.

For carrying wounded men, the best way is to take two light poles, about nine feet long, lash on a couple of cross sticks, about two feet long, and fasten to the poles some tent cloth, or a blanket. If the distance is great, and you cannot obtain a conveyance, you can use horses or mules, by taking longer and stronger poles, the ends of which you use for thills, and harness a horse between them at each end, the patient lying in the blanket in the center.

After the first three days of camp life, many suffer with a dull headache, and a vague dull oppression of the internal organs. This is a disturbance of the system, something akin to biliousness, and is probably owing to a change in one's habits of life. It will soon wear away of itself, but the whole trouble can be readily removed by taking five grains of blue pill, to be followed a few hours afterward by quinine, fifteen grains of which are to be taken in twenty-four hours, in doses of three grains each.

MALARIA.

Avoid marshes and stagnant water as much as possible during the hot months, as it may produce ague. Ague is marked first by a chill, which in about an hour gives way to a fever, followed by a sweat. These symptoms repeat themselves, the next, or second day after, at the same hour.

For treatment, take in the course of twenty-four hours, flfteen grains of quinine, in five doses, of three grains each. (Pills will be the most convenient to carry). This will almost always stop the attack; but as the ague has a tendency to return in a week or two, it is best to take three pills a day for two weeks as a preventive.

DIARRHŒA.

Cholera morbus generally comes on in consequence of indiscretion in eating. The symptoms are a violent purging, accompanied with vomiting. For treatment the patient should wrap up well in blankets, and keep perfectly quiet, lying in a horizontal position. Take a teaspoonful of paregoric in a little water every hour as long as the vomiting continues; when that ceases, if the diarrhœa continues, take a teaspoonful of paregoric every two hours.

For ordinary diarrhœa, take a teaspoonful of paregoric every two or three hours.

Dysentery is a diarrhœa accompanied with discharges of blood and slime, with painful straining; it can be treated in the same way as the ordinary diarrhœa.

If from the effects of paregoric the patient becomes drowsy, lessen the dose, or omit it entirely.

Essence of ginger is an excellent remedy for slight diarrhœa. Take a teaspoonful in a little water two or three times a day. A few drops of camphor on sugar, or in a little water, at intervals of half an hour, will frequently check the disease.

All the above prescriptions are for adults. Children require smaller doses, according to their age and constitutions: judgment must be used. A general rule is, that a dose for a child is in the same proportion to an adult's dose, as the weight of the child compared to the weight of an adult.

For all bowel complaints, it is advisable to wrap a piece of flannel across the bowels. If you do not have any flannel, take a summer under-wrapper and fold it up and place it over the bowels, using the sleeves to fasten behind, so as to keep it in place.

For any poison taken internally, a powerful emetic should be given as soon as possible. A large teaspoonful of ground mustard stirred in water (a coffee cup full) to which may be added a teaspoonful of salt—

makes a good emetic. The mustard should be fresh ; if not, then use a larger quantity.

Where opiates have been used to excess, a cup of very strong coffee should be given as an antidote, and the patient should be kept roused and active by slapping and walking him around till the effects of the opiate are overcome.

DROWNING.

In cases of drowning, *first get air into the lungs as soon as possible.* There is often much loss of time, resulting fatally, by not bearing this in mind. Generally there is no water in the lungs, but a little in the mouth, which can be allowed to run out ; that in the stomach is of no consequence. Hot bottles, rubbing, and other appliances are all useful in their way, but all these are *secondary*, and they cause loss of precious time. On the average a person will expire from loss of air in four minutes ; therefore, the *first* thing is to get air into the lungs. To accomplish this, lay the patient on his back, and alternately expand and depress the chest by taking hold of the arms between the wrist and the elbow, and extending the arms straight out and a little backward, sweeping them up beside the head, but not so violently as to strain the person ; then depress the arms quickly, so that the elbows touch each other close down on, and depressing the chest. This motion should be repeated from seventeen to eighteen times a a minute, and care should be taken not to be too violent in your treatment. Although most drowned persons will be past help when five minutes have passed without any breathing, yet there are exceptional cases that hold life much longer. Therefore, if there is the least hope, the above efforts to introduce air should be instantly commenced, and continued a long time.

CHAPTER XIV.

CAMP PHOTOGRAPHY.

THE rapid advance made in the art of photography in the last five years has placed within the reach of the camper, not only a most interesting source of amusement and recreation, but also a very practical and valuable aid in many ways.

Cameras with their accompaniments can be had ranging in price all the way from ten to fifty dollars. But ten dollars buys a complete first-class apparatus for photographic field work (4×5 inch pictures), and views taken by yourself can be had all mounted on cardboard at a cost of from ten to fifteen cents a picture. The marvelous cheapness of this outfit is only equaled by its simplicity.

With the exception of the tripod, the whole outfit goes in a wooden box $9\frac{1}{2} \times 7\frac{1}{2} \times 7\frac{1}{4}$ inches; the tripod folds neatly together and when folded occupies $28 \times 2\frac{1}{2} \times 1\frac{3}{4}$ inches; the box packed and the tripod weigh together between six and seven pounds.

The above dimensions are for an outfit making a picture 4×5 inches, which is a favorite size for general miscellaneous work. The 5×8 plate gives a larger picture, and on some accounts is preferable. This equipment packed occupies, however, nearly twice the dimensions given above.

Dry plates are used, thus obviating all necessity for taking chemicals with you. Moreover these dry plates, containing the views which you have taken, can be developed, and the photographs mounted upon reaching home by a photographer at the cost mentioned above, in case you do not wish to do that portion of the work yourself. But the whole process from the taking of the picture upon the "dry plate" to its mounting upon the cardboard is now made so simple and easy that any young person can easily understand it with a little reading and a few experiments. Ladies will have no difficulty in using the instrument, and will find it a source of much enjoyment.

To the artist who desires to retain a perfect outline of some view or to reproduce nature upon the spot, for future studies; to the naturalist too far from civilization to retain fresh specimens for preservation; to the geologist and to the botanist this little instrument will prove most valuable. And who of us, not being artists, have not wished for the power to reproduce for our own pleasure and enjoyment in after days, some camp scene by the river side or some secret nook or quiet brook. Modern science has made it possible for everyone to take accurate and permanent pictures. And certainly for the entertainment of those at home or for the purpose of refreshing remembrances of camp scenes and incidents, amateur photography is one of the camper's best friends. It is practical, useful in very many ways, convenient, and not expensive.

There are a number of "outfits" furnished by different houses, and slightly varying in requisites, price, etc. For a camp outfit, the following articles are required: A camera, plate-holder, lens, carrying-case, and tripod, all of which are included for ten dollars, and in addition to these, must be added a focusing cloth, (price $1), a light-tight negative box, (price sixty-five cents), a ruby lantern, (price fifty cents), or dark bag, and gelatine dry plates, (price ninety-five cents per dozen, 4×5 inches).

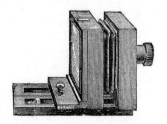

Cameras are of different sizes, adapted to receiving plates which run in the following order: 2½×3¼, 4×5, 5×8, 6½×8½, 8×10, 10×12, 11×14, 14×17 inches, and so on.

Tripods are generally made to fold; but those which have a sliding attachment are superior, though a little higher in price.

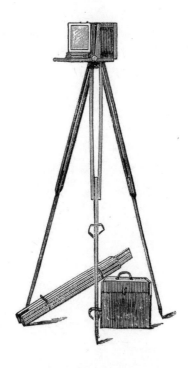

Focusing cloths should be of very dark color or black, and about two by three feet in size. The expense of purchasing one can be avoided by cutting up an old piece of velveteen or black muslin. They can be had of rubber, which will be found convenient in case of rain; and with a little care and ingenuity a dark room, or tent, can be made by arranging it over the tripod.

A pocket magnifying glass will be found a useful aid in focusing; and a very small spirit level will assist in determining the correct position of the camera.

The gelatine dry plate is extremely sensitive to white light, and must not be allowed to come in contact with it for a moment. Even moonlight will affect it. Therefore, in removing the plates from the packages to the plate-holder, or from the plate-holder to the negative box, great care should be exercised that this is done in a dark closet or room from which every ray of *white* light has been totally excluded. You work by the light of a lantern which gives a ruby or red light. If great care is used in closing your tent, you can make the requisite changes at night in that by the light of the ruby lantern.

The plates should be handled by touching the edges only, and to one accustomed to it the changing of the plates can be made, even in the daytime, in the field by the use of a dark bag. This bag should be sufficiently large to hold the negative box and plate holder, and allow freedom of movement. It is best made of thick material of red or orange color, and should have an elastic ribbon at the top. It is also a good plan to have a cloth between the arms when using the bag, so as to further prevent light from entering at the mouth.

A double plate holder carries two plates, which allows the taking of two different views before changing plates. By purchasing an extra double plate holder one is prepared to take four pictures, which can be left in the holders till the return home. If however it is desired to take quite a number of views on the excursion, one is under the necessity of taking more holders, which on account of expense and inconvenience is objectionable, or else of frequently changing the plates. It will therefore be well to make some experiments in changing plates, both with the bag and in the tent at night, before leaving home. Also, if possible, take one or two lessons from some practical photographer.

In the making of photographs by the dry plate process, there are three divisions : first, producing the negative, the requisites for which have already been given ; second, the development of the negative ; third, the printing of the photograph. Unless one has plenty of time, and is especially desirous of doing his own work, the second and third divisions had best be left to a practical photographer, who, upon being furnished with the negatives, will supply photographs by the dozen at a comparatively small cost.

For those who desire, however, to do everything themselves, the following will be sufficient material for furnishing over a hundred photographs four by five inches in size, viz :

FOR DEVELOPING NEGATIVES.

2 4 × 5 japanned pans,
1 4 oz. graduate,
1 set 5 in. japanned scales and weights,
1 oz. bromide ammonium,
1 lb. neutral oxalate potash,
1 lb. protosulph. iron,

1 lb. alum,
1 bottle of varnish,
1 dozen 4 × 5 dry plates,
1 focusing cloth,
1 ruby lantern,
1 oz. sulphuric acid,
1 lb. hyposulph. soda.

(Price $6.50, packed in wooden case.)

FOR PRINTING THE SAME.

1 4 × 5 printing frame,
1 5 × 7 porcelain pan, deep,
1 4½ × 5½ tray,
8 dozen 4 × 5 sensitized albumen paper,
1 bottle No. 1, for toning,
1 bottle No. 2, " "
1 2-ounce graduate.

1 lb. hyposulph. soda,
2 dozen sheets 6½ × 8½ cardboard with gilt form,
1 1½ pint jar parlor paste,
1 ½ inch bristle brush.
1 glass form (for trimming prints),
1 Robinson's straight trimmer.

(Price, securely packed in paper box, about $5.)

While we think amateur photography well worthy the attention of the camper, it will hardly be within the scope of this work to more than briefly touch upon the subject.

The process as now used, is so simple that it can be easily mastered, yet instruction upon so technical a subject should be given by an expert. We therefore refer the reader to two excellent little manuals, the one by Henry Clay Price, entitled "How to make pictures," a very comprehensive work; the other "The Photographic Amateur," by J. T. Taylor.

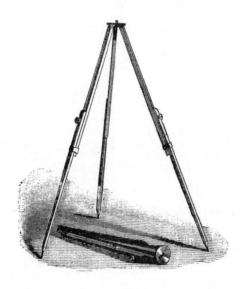